AF263615

We are Australian

A living history

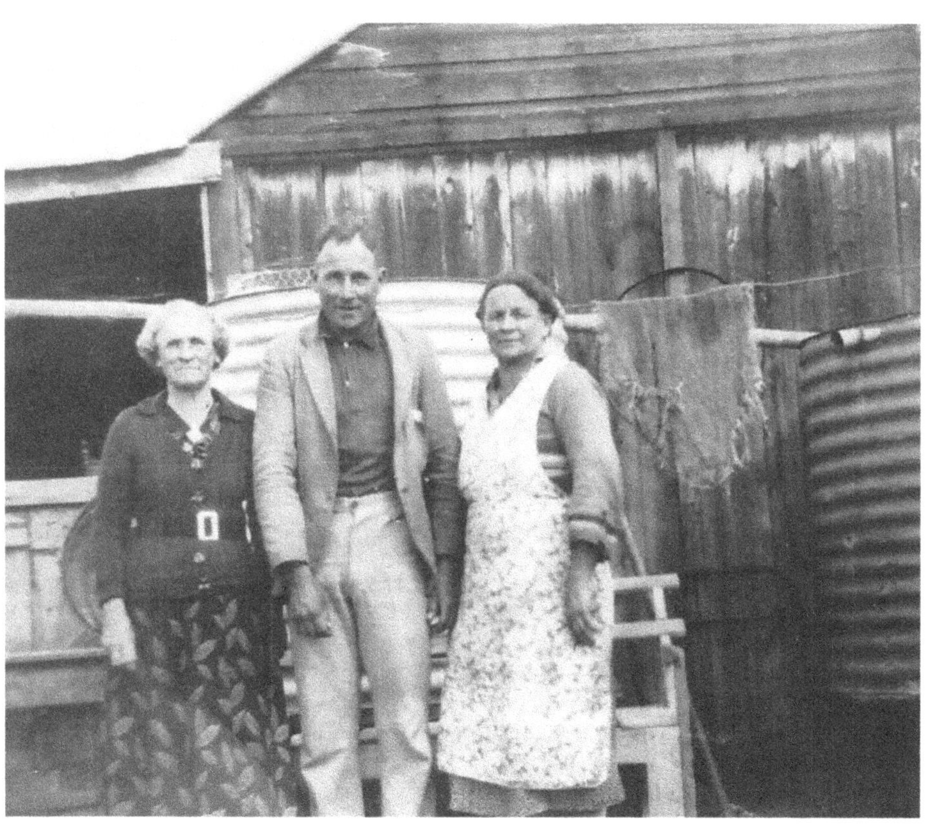

Stories of Australian life by Aussies

Copyright ©2010 Magdalena Ball; © Christina Batey; ©Rachel Bennet; ©Louise Berry; © Linda Ruth Brooks; © Julie Cochrane; © Adam Cope; ©Les Cope; © Jennifer Goard; © Jo Hanrahan; © Gail Hennessy; © Roslyn Jewel; ©John McBride; ©Victoria Norton; © Rina Robinson; ©Jo Tregellis; © Linda Visman; © Matthew Glenn Ward

All rights reserved. This book is copyright protected. Apart from any fair dealings for the purpose of private study, criticism, research or review as permitted under the *Copyright Act (Australia),* no part may be reproduced by any process without written permission. Enquiries should be addressed to the publisher.

Australiana/Australian history/memoir

Project Manager & Publisher– Linda Brooks
General Editor – Linda Visman; Associate Editor – Gail Hennessy

Art for Aftermath of war, People and Community, Christmas– Linda Brooks
Art for Home and Family – Steve James
Art for Place – Les Cope
Cover & interior design - Linda Brooks
Cover photograph – Linda Brooks
Back cover story by John McBride

ISBN: 978-0-9808161-6-7

A copy of this book can be found in the National Library of Australia.

The authors in this book have attempted to recall events to the best of their memory. At times, names and places have been changed, and some minor facts may have been altered to protect others. By their inclusion here, each author and artist claims and maintains individual copyright of their work/s. This includes the right to publish their individual works in any other publication. Individual contributors are legally liable for their own content; no personal responsibility is accepted by the publisher. Every attempt has been made by authors to give appropriate acknowledgments for their material, visual or written.

Place

Christmas

Foreword

Having relatives living on the other side of our great continent provided me with very long journeys in order to visit them. My finances meant these journeys were often undertaken by coach.

Three days is a long time to spend in the company of strangers. With my older son being only three, it would be reasonable to assume this made those journeys hell. However due to his propensity to find any transport movement hypnotic and his patient nature, the opposite was true—he travelled better than I did.

He made friends with most of the other travellers, learning string tricks from an American tourist and generally conversing with anyone who would listen. I often awoke to find he had exchanged seats and was cheerfully holding court at the other end of the coach. On one such occasion I woke to find an elegant blonde woman in the seat beside me. She looked like she'd just stepped off the cover of a Vogue fashion magazine.

'Your son is very persuasive,' she said with a warm smile.

'Oh dear,' I murmured, looking around for his new location.

'He's fine. I think he's working his way through a packet of pineapple lollies with a group of Army recruits.'

I found that was just what he was doing. No doubt along with regaling them with some embarrassing story of his mother, who wasn't like other mothers.

The woman and I shared our lives in the manner of strangers who will never see each other again. I was surprised to learn she was an archaeologist. Being before the days of Harrison Ford and the glamorising of archaeological digs, I'm afraid I viewed this news as rather boring—until she began to talk about her work.

She was obviously passionate about her career and I gained new insight into her world. It had been my perception that most archaeological excavations were centred on unearthing treasures of gold and immense financial worth.

However, I found the most important 'finds' were simple things, revealing the communal life of the times. It made sense. After all, very few of the populace were pharaohs, kings or titled gentry. She spoke of the joy of discovering broken cooking pots, tools of trade and religious symbols. I learned true history is about everyday life.

Nationhood was built on simpler things than I'd first thought, and these discoveries formed a view of the past. It is precisely why the stories in this anthology are important—as living history. In them we learn about simple pleasures, such as Jaffas at the movies, the age of Rock'n'Roll, the magic of blended culture through two tone shoes, the rites of religious passage of a young girl fervently praying the rosary for her sick father and brother.

We laugh when the Christmas pudding catches on fire, when neighbourhood thugs find karma in the suburbs and when a first sailing adventure faces disaster. Earthquake, a National Disaster Area and a volcano are all here. Along with friendships, partings, love and estrangement—the gamut of the human experience.

We meet an indigenous family fighting to learn the truth about a loved one's death while serving his country. A son remembers a war-weary father who marched the Kokoda Trail, and a mother shares the joy of her three children. We pay tribute to the Stolen Generation and warriors defending the gentle giants of the sea—our whales. We share the love of a wife requesting her husband's surgeon to take care of her lover's heart and a family's devotion to a disabled son, with a unique gift for poetry, and deep insights into life.

We read about the innocent joys of childhood, the love of grandparents and the extended family. So, here we are to share the kitchen pots, the tools of trade, the building of homes, living with hardship and the experience of integrating with other cultures. We hope that you will enjoy these stories and the journey back along memory lane, and realise that we are all a part of life's 'living history'.

Linda Brooks

Aftermath of war

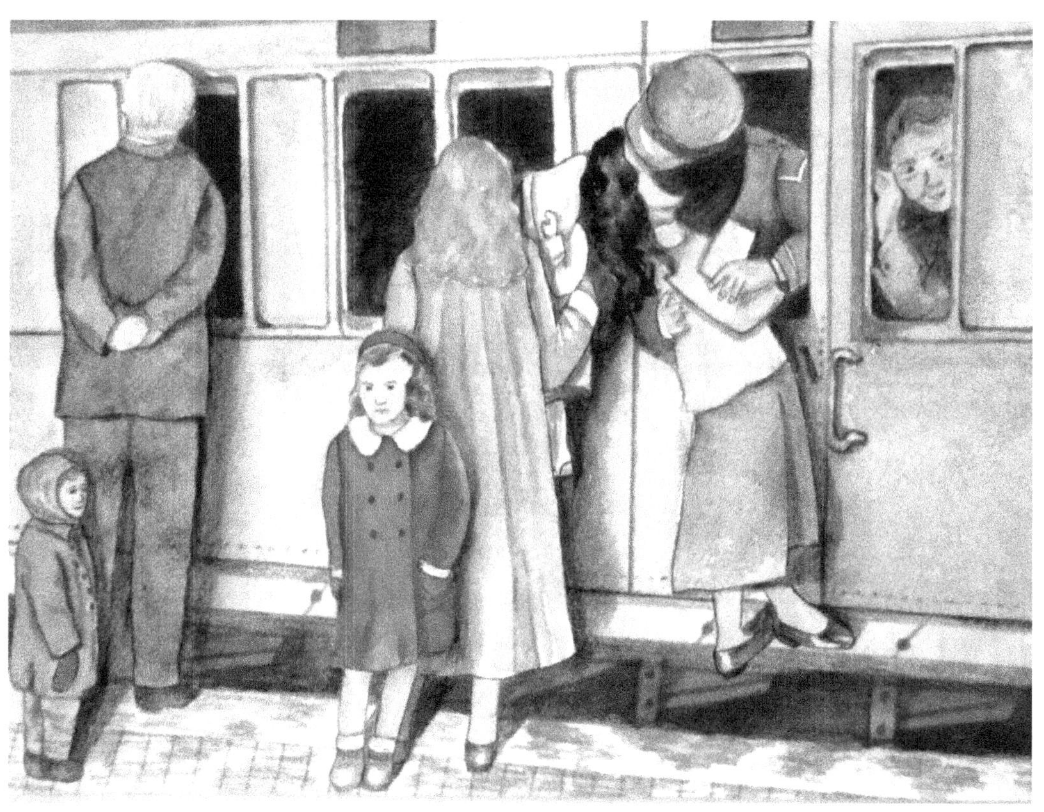

6.00am, Chelsea railway station, Melbourne.

Winter shrouds the morning with her coat of cold, grey rain, the huge crystal drops attempting to drench all who venture out into her harsh embrace.

A lonely figure stands next to the ticket machine on the sheltered ramp leading onto the station. His bluey jacket, denim jeans and Blundstones are all that stands between him and the elements. He carries his tray suspended on a strap around his neck. A crowd of people rush up the ramp toward him, hurrying to catch the train which will take them into the city for work. Heads are bent against the pelting rain, umbrellas closing as they reach the shelter of the stations' roof.

'I'll buy a five dollar badge from you mate,' says an elderly chap in a dark suit, his newspaper tucked under his arm to read on the train.

'No worries,' Ted replies. He pulls a little metal pin badge from his tray. Yellow is the colour of the five dollar one, blue is for ten, green is for twenty and the two dollar ones are red. The little badges are stuck into bits of foam in their relevant denomination and look just like soldiers on a parade ground standing to attention.

In his right hand Ted holds a money collection tin with a single word describing his cause stuck onto the front of it; this word has also been embroidered onto his peaked hat. Ted's pride for his mission shines from his eyes. It is easy to see his heart is in this task.

'I'll have a ten dollar one please,' says woman handing over her money, 'My grandma was a Legacy widow. Thanks.' She rushes onto the platform to board the train.

Ted's grey hair sticks out from underneath his hat. Once upon a time his hair was the colour of night, his face had fewer lines and his eyes saw much more than they do now. He was in the Australian Navy and like so many others of our nation he went to war. His generation went to action in Vietnam and saw mates become injured in combat. Some paid the ultimate price for their deeds with their lives. Ted's grandfather, Bill, saw the sands of Gallipoli first hand and ended up on the Somme. He came home, a changed and shattered man who found solace in alcohol. No-body understood the effect war had on people when Ted's grandfather came home from France. Bill's wife had died while he was away and his five sons were split up around the country. The effect the Great War had on Ted's grandfather's family was a common occurrence. Who would look after the kids?

Bill did a stint in HM Prison Pentridge for vagrancy and died a very unheroic death, drowning his body and mind in alcohol, a victim of war. Ted's dad, who shared his father's name, Bill, although he signed on, never made it to WWII. He lost the fingers on his right hand in an accident. Surprisingly the Army wouldn't let him go overseas, because he couldn't fire a weapon. He spent the war at home driving trucks for the Army. He too found solace in alcohol.

When Ted came home from Vietnam it was to a hostile Australian public. Vietnam was unlike WWI and II. Sure men still returned home, wounded, maimed for life or in a pine box, but support for this war had waned. People were angry that once again their husbands, sons and brothers were dying in someone else's country, in someone else's war.

The response to the returned servicemen in the ANZAC Day parade in Melbourne after Vietnam was hurtful to say the least. People who lined the streets spat at the men marching. Curses, death threats and swearing followed the servicemen up St Kilda road to The Shrine of Remembrance. It was hardly a fitting homecoming for those who had no say in a war they were sent to fight.

Ted cried that day. I had never seen a grown man cry. He came home with a bellyful of alcohol, lay face down on his bed, and cried tears of shame, humiliation and sorrow. He was a lucky bloke like his father and grandfather—they came home.

Countless men, war after war, buried their fallen comrades with many a promise made in the heat of the moment. 'Who will look after my wife and kids?' The fallen whisper, their ghostly voices combining in a chorus of concern.

'Don't worry mate,' came the reply, 'I'll carry that legacy for you.'

8:00 am, and Ted's stint at the station has finished. He has spoken to numerous travellers and has sold many little badges, all bearing the same word, 'Legacy'.

He closes his box of badges and heads out into the rain soaked morning. His spot will be taken up by another bloke ready to help raise money for the war torn families of Australia.

These lucky men, who came back, who didn't die on the battle field are the silent heroes. Yes, their brothers in arms are remembered in our histories – and rightly so – for dying in major battles which saved our way of life. But it must have been so hard for the men who came home to move into – what we civvies call – normality.

Even though the ones who remain grow older, it's nice to know that they care enough to want to help the ones who were left behind.

Air Raid Shelter - Gail Hennessy

I'd fashioned houses in caves,
under seaside scrub.
My father blasted
through a shelf of rock
a cubby house deluxe.

I dreamt war games
longing for sirens
stalking through shivery
grass, somersaulting
trenches
conjuring cannon fire.

Peace, and the shelter
held rain water
in a chalice of retribution.

My father filled it in.

The grass crept over
like a patch in my mother's
eiderdown, quilting the garden
the land never quite healing.

He was young and built like a bull; tireless, massive and strong, but protective and gentle. Gordon Stockdale was my mother's brother, and a marvellous human being who showed me unconditional love all his life. There was room in his heart for all.

He never walked away from a fight, but he never started one. One thoughtless man who challenged him to a fight was thrown unceremoniously up on the head-high wheat bales at the factory where he worked. The fight was over without a punch. Walking off without a word or a backward glance he continued with his tasks.

During World War II he marched the Kokoda trail; for his country, and for his mother and seven siblings. His father, Joe Stockdale, had died while working with my Uncle Gordon while they were cutting and carrying rail sleepers. Joe was also a man of immense strength, but his heart collapsed with the heavy labour.

They were alone in the early morning mist of the mountains. Uncle Gordon broke down in tears when he saw the beginning of the movie, 'The Man from Snowy River'. He relived that terrible day.

While he was serving as a medic in Papua New Guinea every penny of his wage was sent home to his mother. Never faltering, he lived life at the same pace every day. Riding a motorcycle at well below the speed limit earned him the nickname of 'Speed Gordon'. He never raced or competed with anyone. A master at word games, he parried without arguing.

He walked miles for his church and his God. With a smile as broad as his shoulders he gave crushing handshakes—they became his trademark. Many a younger man jostled to prove themselves by shaking his strong hands, but all walked away nursing their bruises. For many years he stood at the top of the church steps to welcome anyone to God's house. Wearing the same kind of boots his whole life, he always walked for someone else - mowing lawns for 'the dear old ones' when he himself was over 80.

After he met plain, gentle Alice, he married the love of his life, the heart and soul of his kitchen and his home. It was truly a humble home and he spent the whole of his life paying it off at the same pace. No more or less than the repayment amount on the low interest war loan he was awarded on his return from the war, making the final payment when he was about 82. The simple life was enough for this truly humble man. He deplored pretentiousness of any sort—it was unmanly. Tenderly caring for Alice and his orchids, he never sought to advance his career or his lifestyle.

They never had children, and as a tiny girl this worried me. I was sad for him. I knew he had fought in The War. I didn't know his rank or position; to me he was 'Gorgie'. All his life he was a hard working man - I remember him saying, 'I'd like to die with my boots on'.

'Why don't you have any little girls or boys, Gorgie?' I once asked, as I sat in my usual place—on his strong knees on the back steps of their home.

'I never wanted sons for cannon fodder,' he replied. His eyes had a faraway look.

I tilted my head. I didn't understand. He ruffled my curls.

'I can be your little girl, Gorgie. Mum and Dad won't mind sharing,' I offered.

'You're already my little girl. Why, we have the same birthday, so that seals it.'

Every year on our birthday I'd get up early. Searching through Mum's stationery cupboard I'd find some used wrapping paper. I'd steal one of Dad's handkerchiefs and wrap it into an awkward lump. Then the race was on. They lived half a mile up the street and I would try and beat Uncle Gordon to his back door before he arrived at our house. It was many years before I made it to his house first. My gifts had improved by then, which was just as well because Mum had noticed the alarming 'disappearance' of Dad's handkerchiefs. By Dad's subtle winks it was clear he knew, but he said nothing.

'Never known a man to lose so many blooming handkerchiefs, Max.'

'Beats me Else,' he responded blandly. 'How many men with handkerchiefs have you known Else?'

'Pfft.'

It was a long time before I understood what Uncle Gordon meant about cannon fodder. He explained a little more about the war as I grew older, and gave more insights when I began my nurse's training. It was at the birth of my first son, Luke, when the reality dawned on me—the overwhelming vulnerability life brings you when you love someone that much. You can be undone in a minute. You may have lived the early years of your life strong and invincible, but when you had created life and held a son in your arms it was different. For a man who'd seen so much 'wasted manhood' it was more than he could imagine surviving.

Letting me into his world he talked of his time working as a medic in the army Hospital in New Guinea; of the crashing grief he felt the day he'd been told his best friend had been hit. Desolate and stricken, he went out to look for his friend, but there was nothing of his they could recognize. Cannon fodder. He told me of the nervous breakdown he suffered many years after his return from the war, and how it had made him seek and enjoy the simple life so fervently.

Alice patiently gave me gourmet cooking lessons. When she died he gave the Kenwood to me. I worshipped it. I had it for many years before it stopped. One morning he asked if I would take him shopping. He limped through David Jones in his boots, favouring his painful leg; pain caused by the prostate cancer that was taking over his body. He went to the girl at the checkout and threw down a pile of fifty dollar notes. The sales girl was taken aback.

'I would like the best Kenwood Mixmaster you have, my dear. Thank you kindly.' Tears pricked my eyes—so that was the purpose of our shopping day. I still have that Kenwood.

And then, with the same courage that he faced every other journey in life, he faced death. He was sick from the morphine when he came to visit one holiday and I was morning sick.

I went with him to pathology and radiology. The radiologist asked me to come into the room to be with him, because his kidneys were so diseased. It was taking a long time for the dye to run through for them to get a scan, so I went in the radiology room and I knelt beside him. We talked of nothing; something. Mostly, he worried about me kneeling there too long.

I visited him after his first heart attack, driving five hours to see him. When I arrived at the hospital I found him in the general ward, clutching his chest in pain, lips blue with lack of oxygen, unshaven and unwashed. I was furious.

'Why is my uncle in pain?' I asked the nursing staff. My eyes were fierce.

'We've given him something.' They told me what they'd given.

'That would possibly be enough for a small animal!' I said. 'He's a huge man. He's clutching his chest. It's five hours since that piddling dose. This is a man who marched the Kokoda Track—a man who bought the freedom you now enjoy. Your world is different because of men like him. I don't care if you don't string him up to every monitor in the place or shave him before lunch time, but you will never leave my uncle in pain again.'

I shaved him and washed his face and hands. He squeezed my hand.

'Ouch, don't crush me, Gorgie.' I shook my hand in mock pain. He smiled weakly.

'In all the years I fought for others, I never thought I'd need someone to fight for me. And I certainly never expected it to be the one who sat on my knee promising to be 'my little girl'.'

'Then I am privileged.'

'No my dear, I am.'

The nurses called me 'Matron', but after that he was comfortable and clean.

He died four days after our mutual birthday and three days before my youngest son was born. Maybe it takes three days to get to heaven. Maybe he'd been called for 'guardian angel' duty.

I remember the Kokoda Track - John McBride

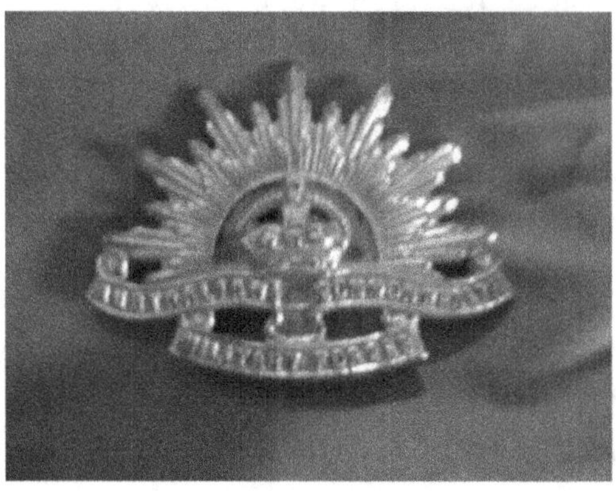

I remember when I was very young, seeing the military great-coat hanging on a nail in the room at the back of the house. This room, called the 'wash-room', contained the copper, scrubbing brush, shoe brush and polish, and other knick-knacks. On a nail behind the door, half hidden by what we called the 'old rag bag' hung a khaki great coat, with a single stripe on the arm and an oval-shaped emblem signifying my father's battalion.

I remember at Christmas time, we thought we were the luckiest children alive. Every year we went to two Christmas parties. One was held on a Saturday afternoon. It was organised by my dad's work, and was called the Maples Christmas party. Why we were lucky was that, when our name was called out, we walked up and received a wrapped present from Father Christmas. The other party was always on a Friday evening. It was held at a military barracks, down in Batman Avenue, I think. I remember it being near Olympic Park, as we walked along the edge of Olympic Park to get there. It was the 39th Battalion Christmas Party. It was held in a hall. At one end, just in front of the stage was a flag on a pole- the flag had the same emblem that hung on the great coat.

I remember as a small child hearing the grownups refer in their conversations to The Blackout, and events that happened 'during the blackout'.

I remember around the corner from our house in Northcote, in the adjoining street, McCracken Avenue, there was a sign on a lamp post saying 'This is a War Savings Street'.

I remember at family parties and gatherings the grownups talked about the good times, the hilarious and major things that happened at a time called 'The end of the war'. I remember as a small child, having a romantic notion of this wonderful time called 'the end of the war'.

I remember on Anzac Day, we would sometimes visit other people's houses. Some years the people we visited had Television, and on Anzac Day it would show documentaries about the war.

The film footage always seemed to show ships at sea and aircraft taking off.

I remember when I was ten, getting angry at my mother and calling her a name. I don't remember what the name was; but all of a sudden I felt a blow and went sprawling across the room. I looked up in pain and my father was standing there, red in the face and shaking.

I remember occasionally we would be at someone's house and could hear adults talk. A man would nod in my father's direction and say, 'That's Jack. He was in the 39th Battalion'.

I remember my Uncle John called around one evening with a book by an author named Raymond Paul, titled 'Retreat from Kokoda'. My mum and Uncle John were quite excited; but Dad ignored it all and kept on playing Euchre with Grandpa. Next morning when I got up, the book was still sitting on the kitchen table.

I remember taking the book and speed reading through every page. On page 42, it said , 'At Awala, three days later. Collyer reported to Templeton, proceeding with Pte John McBride from Kokoda to Buna. They returned to Awala on 21st July. As they rested there from the heat, they heard but disregarded a distant rumbling noise which seemed to emanate from the massive banks of clouds, the seat of tropical thunder, in the direction of the coast'.

I remember sitting there in the kitchen and thinking about my dad, resting in the jungle and hearing the sound like thunder in the distance. I remember the magic and the romance and the pride, as I sat there a small boy, at the kitchen table in Northcote.

I remember when a teenager, occasionally there would be a story in the Sun newspaper about the Kokoda Track. My mother would cut it out and paste it in an exercise book.

I remember as a teenager watching the Anzac Day parade on television, and getting a thrill when they described the 'heroes' of the 39th Battalion as they proudly marched past. I also remember that Dad never showed any interest in going to the Anzac Day parade.

I remember, one day when the family was together around a picnic table, I told a story. 'One day a boy dropped his watch over the side of a boat when at sea. Years later, he was at the kitchen table preparing a fish to cook for tea and the knife he was holding cut into something hard - it was his thumb.' I heard a sound, looked up and saw my father laughing.

I remember as an adult, many years later when my father died that was the only time I had ever seen him laugh.

I remember as I grew older, the references to the Kokoda Track became more and more frequent at family gatherings, and there were more and more occasions where people pointed out my father to neighbours and cousins and told about the 39th Battalion.

I remember none of those conversations ever included Dad. He was in the distance, and was whispered about.

I remember when I was about thirty years old; I visited my parents one evening with my wife and young family. I was about to go to Japan for a scientific conference. My father acted very uneasy, and said he did not like me going to Japan. I tried to question him and explore his objection; but he would not talk.

I remember the day my father died. My wife, children and I were visiting my parents for Sunday lunch. On the way across the suburbs we stopped at the Camberwell market; so we arrived at lunch a little late. When we arrived, there were several cars around my parents' house. My brother Adrian answered the door. I asked what he was doing there, and he told me 'Dad died this morning.'

I remember about fifteen years later, Mum died. Society had changed then such that at funerals it had become common for a member of the family to give a eulogy during the funeral. I sat up during the night working hard, using all the professional skills acquired over the years in my profession, trying to write a eulogy that did justice to my mother.

The eulogy was a description of my mother's life; and my delivery took 20 to 30 minutes. Near the start I mentioned that she met my father before the beginning of the war; that at Christmas time 1941 he left for New Guinea; he was a member of a famous Battalion that was massacred and reformed several times; and that he spent the entire war on the frontline in New Guinea, at one stage having been declared 'missing in action', and that he travelled home in 1945 to marry my mother. Throughout my childhood their black and white wedding photo stood proudly in a frame on their bedroom dresser, with Dad in his military uniform. In the eulogy I mentioned he was always ill after the war, but that he struggled to work at the furniture shop in Smith St Fitzroy, until finally in the seventies he was declared Totally and Permanently Incapacitated (TPI) resulting from his war service; and was pensioned off until his death in 1981. This was a very small part of my mother's eulogy taking a few minutes. The complete address had a very different emphasis and went on for 20 to 30 minutes.

I remember after the funeral, standing in the foyer of the church while friends and well-wishers came up and grasped me and comforted me. My cousin Lester said the words about my father and the war meant a lot to him: 'That bloody war,' he said. 'I grew up with a father sitting inside and not talking to us'. Then another male friend stopped by and told essentially the same story; then another… so I was standing there in an emotional state thinking we were an entire generation who grew up with fathers who were physically present, but whose minds were far away.

I remember visiting my father's grave many years later, with my second wife, who had not been there during my middle age, during my father's death, and my mother's death. We drove to the

Preston cemetery and walked through the aisles of graves, and came across a soldier's grave, low-lying and unadorned, with my name on it: 'Sergeant John McBride'. And in gold engraving was that same symbol of the rising sun that I saw on the great coat and in the sewing machine drawers all those years before. I remember not being able to speak, my voice choking, with my new and younger wife wondering why I cried so long and so hard simply when visiting a cemetery.

I remember only a few months ago walking through a bookshop in town with my 19 year old daughter (who lives with her mother). On the display-stand at the front of the shop was a display of a book titled 'Kokoda' with a cover photo of Australian soldiers from my father's era. I said to my daughter, 'I suppose you know your grandfather, my dad, was at Kokoda'. My daughter said, 'No, I didn't know that. I have heard about Kokoda at school many times. I didn't know there was any personal connection'.

I remember buying a book in the Johannesburg Airport, about growing up in South Africa. The style was interesting and unique. The book was titled 'We walk straight so you better get out of the way' by Denis Hirson. Every paragraph of the book began with the phrase 'I remember….' Reading Hirso's book on the plane on my way home from South Africa. As I sat there in Business Class, relaxing and sipping a glass of wine, I had the idea to write this story.

I remember being a 55 year old man, sitting in Business Class on my recliner seat, sipping a glass of wine, with tears rolling down my face … the pain of Kokoda has not finished yet.

1. The Soldier

He was barely twenty
she was almost six.
She had come
from Bidura home
for abandoned children,
she thought him her brother,
he had enlisted
to fight a foreign foe

And told her
don't tell mum.
She did not
want him to leave
and so she stole
the soap
from his kitbag
knew it was wrong

She hid it under the
verandah steps
for was not cleanliness
next to godliness?

Without that
Essential, he was
she believed,
grounded.

After six months
home service
he sailed
for the Western Front

She remembered
the ship
tied to the shore
with streamers
that stretched
and broke.

2. The Mother

On 22 April 1918 a notice from Base Records, London, Australian Imperial Forces, regretted
that her son was wounded:

*It being clearly understood that if no further advice is forwarded this department has no more
information to supply*

Hope still stood
between her and finality.
On 7 May 1918 an urgent telegram
told her of his death.

She wrote in anguish on 20 May seeking clarification …

London answered: *In reply to your communication of the 20th instant I have to state that the date
on which he was wounded is not available. But the latest information to hand shows that he died
of wounds on 4/4/18 (previously reported wounded). No particulars are yet available, but later
official advice coming to hand should contain further details, and these, on receipt, will be
promptly communicated to you.*

The military authorities finally confirmed on 21 October, 1918 he had been killed in action on
4 April 1918 in the attack at Villers-Bretonneux, and did not die of wounds as previously stated.

In those intervening months
his mother had taken his sister
to pubs all over the State

Brandishing his photo
in the hope a returned soldier
would have news of her son.

3. The Sister

My mother
was a young woman
in the kitchen
stoking the fire
when she felt his presence

neither comforting nor scary
she ran next door
to her neighbour
who read the tea leaves

who assured her
he had been there with her,
she carried that memory
all her life for warmth.

4. The Daughter

Some weeks
before she died
my mother told me
she had felt his nearness.

He had come
in a dream
seventy-five years
after his death.

After she died,
in her personal effects
I found one photograph
from my mother's childhood,
a postcard of her brother
serious and serene.

Wearing his slouch hat
member of the Australian
Imperial Forces.

I have nursed war veterans on and off for the past 30 years. During that time I was privileged to have a window into their lives. More often than not, glimpses were all they wanted to give. So now, so many years later, glimpses are all we have. These are a few quotes from veterans in my care over the years.

We were young, we were invincible. Our destination was adventure. We landed in the middle of hell.

You never would have thought it; but the boredom near killed a man at times.

If you weren't there you wouldn't believe it.

There are things a man can't talk about. Only with his mates, the ones who'd been there, and stood shoulder to shoulder with you.

Talking about it just brings back the nightmares. You'd think after all these years a man could lay his head on his pillow and forget.

War changes a man forever. We were different men when we came back.

The waiting was worse. Never knowing where or when or what was around the next bend or tree.

There are things you have to do in war. There are things I had to do I would never tell another human being.

How could you tell your wife and family? They had been through enough carrying on without you. We just got on with life. What else could a man do?

I didn't feel vulnerable or afraid until I came home. Stupid, really.

I came home and thought the world had changed. But I had.

We have invented so many things but we still can't stop men going to war. Until we do we haven't come far as a human race. It's madness, pure and simple.

Some days we weren't men, we were just targets or killing machines.

Family and Home

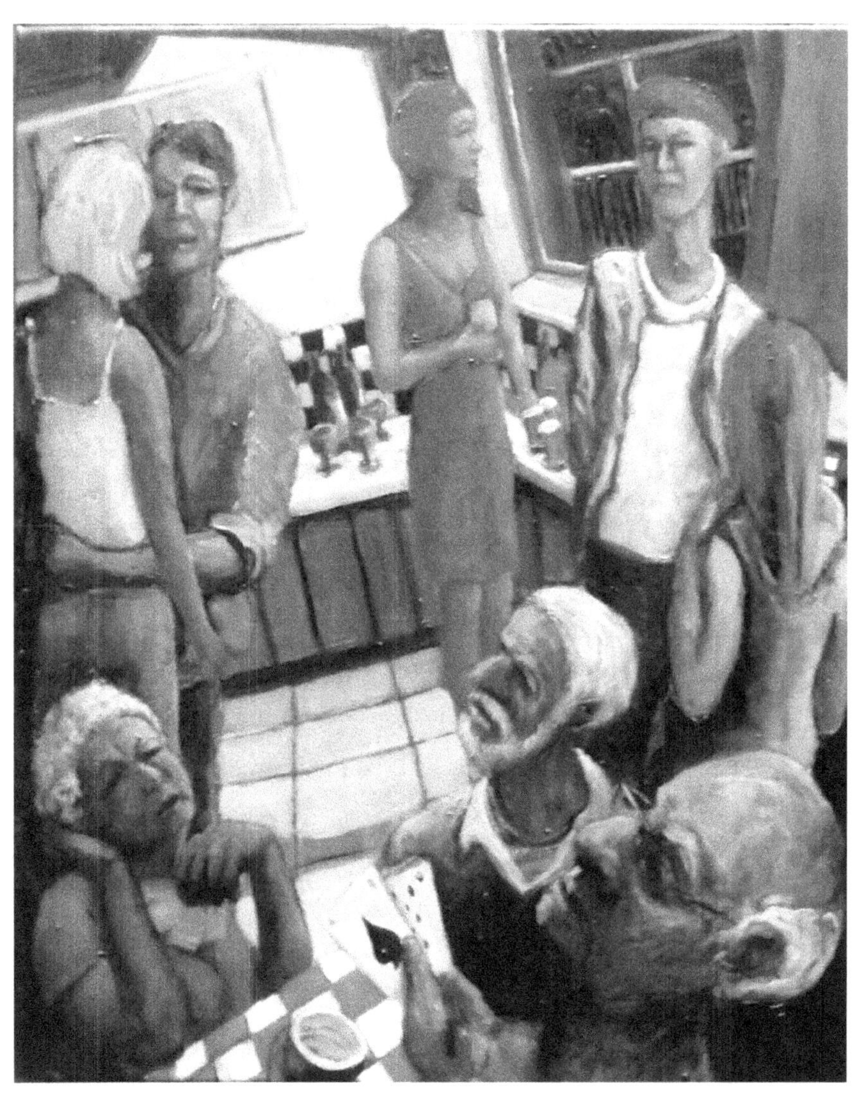

It was at the kitchen table that mum sat - day in day out. She made the pastry on it for the pies and tarts. She flattened dough with a milk bottle instead of a rolling pin. She mixed the cakes on it. She sewed our clothes there, altering our school uniforms. As one of my jobs I had to get the bean slicer out of the cupboard, set it up with the screw mechanism on the edge of the table, and slice the beans.

When we came home after school, mum would be at the kitchen table. We would prepare our slice of bread with vegemite and our glass of milk and Quik and sit at the kitchen table and eat and drink.

In the mornings, we would get up, wash, dress and head down to meet as a family at the kitchen table. We would sit there for brekkie, glancing at the front page of the Sun that always had a large picture of news or fashion. I remember at the kitchen table looking at the picture of Jean Shrimpton in her miniskirt at the Cup, the bushfire tragedies, a soaring big-men-fly mark from the weekend football.

At teatime, we sat as a family at the kitchen table. I had a lot of brothers and sisters, so it was quite a gathering every evening. Occasionally the front door bell would ring in the middle of the meal. We kids never did like that. Mum would collect all our plates into the middle before answering the door. If whoever called was asked to stay, the food was reallocated from the collected plates, so there was enough for the unexpected extra eater.

After tea we would sit at the kitchen table and say the Rosary, before we were sent off to sweep floors, take out the rubbish and do our homework.

On Saturdays I would cook. Dad and I both worked in Smith St. He, on the Fitzroy side at Maples furniture shop, and I was on the Collingwood side at EzyWalkins shoe shop. After work, which in those days was soon after midday, I would walk across to Maples and he would drive us home. Once home, I got out the electric frying pan, mixed the hamburgers, added the egg, and the bacon. Then I would stand there as happy as Larry cooking away while siblings came and went, sitting in turns at the table, while I served them their burgers and eggs. Most Saturdays the Parish Priest would call in, 'Not realising it was meal-time'. We always asked him to stay. I don't remember his name: mum and dad referred to him as the Irish Priest. He always added to the atmosphere of Saturday midday with his strong Irish voice, or brogue…it was so strong that everything he said sounded hilarious.

In the later years, when she grew old, mum would sit at the kitchen table most of the day, listening to talk-back radio on 3AW and reading the Women's Weekly. In the evening she would move into the TV room for a while, but would then gravitate back to the kitchen table for her glass of sherry.

Our kitchen table wasn't much to look at. It had a Laminex top, a shiny silver-appearance rim around the edge, and legs that stuck out at strange angles so they got in the way of anyone who wanted to walk past. I actually don't remember what happened to that original table…tables have evolved and become more modern. Somewhere along the line, someone in the family must have had a look at the kitchen table, decided it was old fashioned, ordered a new one, and chucked it out.

My fondest kitchen-table memories are of Sunday lunch. When we were little, we would usually have guests: cousins, uncles and aunts around to Sunday lunch. We were all dressed in our Sunday-best after going to church. After church, while we waited for people to arrive, we stood out in the front yard, all dressed up, talking to neighbours who went past, and then to the various cousins. The lunch was always something grand: no cheap meat like rabbit or stew – no, we had roast lamb or beef, with dobs of gravy and mashed potato, and in the later years, champagne. The adults told stories and we all laughed.

Thinking back on happy childhood memories, Sunday lunch was as good as it got.

We all grew up and left home.

Dad died.

Soon we had our own kids.

The years went by without the family meeting on a Sunday.

Whenever a family event happened, though, we still met in that kitchen and sat at that table – major birthdays, wedding anniversaries, kids' birthdays.

When dad died, it was on a Sunday. We all gathered, as did all the relatives: the uncles, the aunts, the cousins-they sat in the kitchen, crammed around the table and over cups of tea, glasses of beer and scones, they talked.

Mum and my brothers and sisters were in the lounge room talking with the priest, and then with the funeral director. The funeral director was a bit too suave and smooth for our liking. He produced forms to sign and packages to tell us about.

We had to choose a coffin.

The funeral Director had a glossy book full of the range of possible coffins, with pictures and prices.

'Why don't people just choose the cheap one?' Mum asked. 'After all, it's just going to be down in the ground, covered with dirt.'

'Well…it might give a bad impression,' replied the funeral director. 'You have to ask yourself, what would the relatives think?'

'Ah, that's easy,' said Mum, 'they're all out there at the kitchen table.'

Before the funeral director could react, Mum had grabbed the catalogue of coffins and headed out to the kitchen to ask the relatives what they would think if we chose the cheaper wooden coffin.

Gradually the Sunday lunch came back. I had my own kids and family; so did my brother; so did my sister. We began to meet again at Mum's house on Sunday at lunchtime. And so, after all those years, there we were again, around that same kitchen table.

Then after a while, the bad times began. My mum's sister was diagnosed with cancer: she and the other sister moved in with mum. Mum herself was getting old and had several falls. The first sister died after a very sad year, and almost immediately the second of mum's sisters was diagnosed with cancer; and the whole cycle started again.

These times were bad; but through it all, we met on Sunday at the kitchen table for lunch. There were old people with dementia and with cancer; but we still drank champagne, and had roast lamb or lunch, and the adults told stories. Though now, *we* were the adults.

And for a while there, every Sunday, as we sat around that table, all the bad things happening in our family had gone away.

After another painful year, the second aunt died. Then mum died only a few months after. The family turned on one another through the stress of those times, and among other things we squabbled over possessions: the crystal cabinet, the antique couch that we had in the lounge room. No one wanted the kitchen table though… which is sad when you consider what that table had seen, and what sitting there in the kitchen had meant to us all those years.

And so, the family home was sold at auction one cold, damp Saturday afternoon. It was during a slump in the housing market and we didn't get much for it. After the auction, we headed off to our own homes, to our own kitchens, and to our own kitchen tables. It was a time to take stock and rebuild.

With our second parent having died, we had all grown up now. But, it didn't feel good. At my place, I sat with my wife and children over a cup of tea, at the kitchen table

Sepia Print - Gail Hennessy

I have only one photograph of you
before you were my mother

on a brick edged path you wear
a tailored dress - you always liked tailored

the dress has three pleats which echo
three stanchions of the garden shed behind you

beyond its roof the celery top of a telegraph pole
peers like a future TV aerial of the 50's

tomato stakes in the vegetable bed
stab the air, stitching earth to sky

I can decipher one round tomato
its starred calex sticking fruit to vine

the tomato might be green or pale bronze
or red I don't know the colour

you are bending in an arabesque of care
fondling your Airedale terrier

I witness the dark of your hair
the touch of your hand in the curls of his coat,

in the photo I am not yet your child
though you remain always my mother.

Pray for us, sinners
Linda Visman (October 1961)

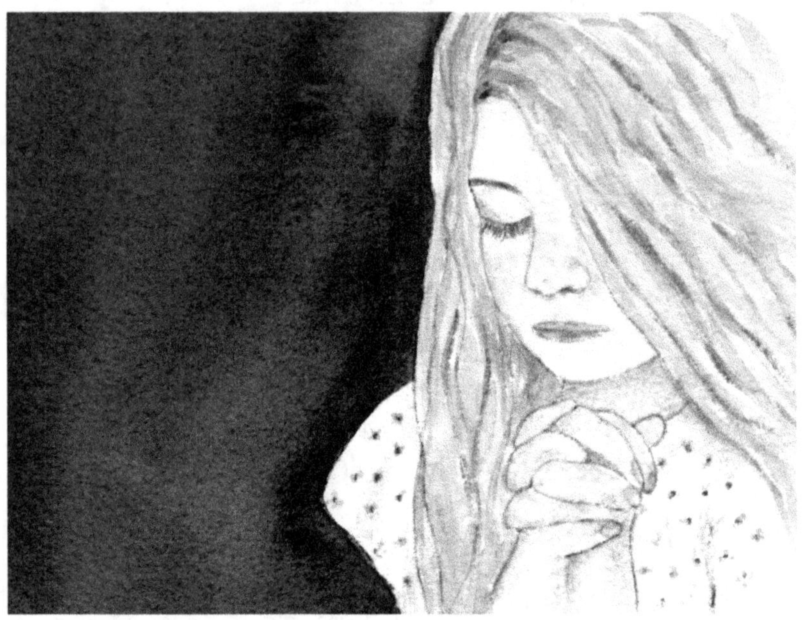

There's a tiny pebble beneath my knee and I open my eyes a fraction. Reaching down, I brush it away, impatient at the distraction. I must keep my concentration total, or my prayers won't be effective.

It's difficult to stay focussed on the Mysteries of the Rosary when I am so worried about Dad. I'm not saying the *Joyful Mysteries*. They don't seem right. Neither do the *Glorious Mysteries*. The *Sorrowful Mysteries* fit the situation much better. The rosary beads pass through my fingers, one for each *Our Father*, ten *Hail Mary*s, and the *Glory be* at the end of each decade of the Rosary. I've done *The Agony in the Garden*. The next decade is *The Scourging at the Pillar*. But my mind refuses to focus on the sufferings of Jesus.

'Please don't let Dad die. Let him come back home soon.'

My concern for my earthly father constantly interrupts my address to the One in Heaven, and again I have to force myself to concentrate.

Hail Mary, full of grace, the Lord is with thee, blessed art thou among women, and blessed is the fruit of thy womb, Jesus. Holy Mary, Mother of God, pray for us, sinners, now and at the hour of our death. Amen.

I can hear my older brother, Peter, in the kitchen. My sisters, Pauline and Sheelagh, are probably there too, though I can't hear them. I'm in the lounge room, in the dark so nobody will see me. I don't know why I don't want them to see me, because we all know how important prayer is – and this is an especially important time for prayer.

The carpet is rough on my knees, but I'm used to kneeling on all sorts of floors. I've done it for most of my thirteen years, and I can ignore the discomfort. However there's usually the back of another pew in church, a desk at school, or my bed to lean against. It's hard to ignore the ache in my back from having no support for most of the *Sorrowful Mysteries*. I stretch, then say another *Hail Mary,* feeling guilty that I can't keep focussed on Jesus and His Mother. My mind soon wanders again.

Mum's at the hospital. I don't know how she got there because there are no buses at night. It's very hard for her. She always worries so much about everything, even little things. Now we have a really big worry. She's already had to go to the hospital every day for the last two weeks to see my little brother, David. Now Dad's in the isolation ward too, in the adults' part, not the kids' part. It's pretty hard for us four as well. We have to wait at home, not knowing what's happening. What will we do if Dad dies?

That's what the prayers are for. Surely Jesus and Mary will help us. We've always gone to Mass and kept the Holy Days. But what if I've done something bad and God won't listen to my prayers? I haven't been able to go to Confession, none of us have. Not since we've been isolated in the house to stop the germs spreading. Surely Jesus will realise that. We can't even go to school. I close my eyes tight and hold my breath, sending my prayers up to Heaven.

'Please listen, God. Even if I've been bad, Daddy's a good man. He loves you and keeps the Commandments and goes to Mass. We don't have much money even though he works hard. Please, don't take him away from us. I'll do anything you want me to.'

Hoping God the Father, Jesus and the Holy Ghost – and Mary too - are all listening, I begin the next decade of the Rosary, *The Crowning with Thorns.* I think about how that must have hurt Jesus. I think about David, and wonder why a three-year-old like him has to suffer.

It was Tuesday two weeks ago, and he was kneeling on the stool at the kitchen sink, playing in the water with his little boats. He wasn't feeling too good and he fell off. Then he couldn't stand up. Mum took him straight to the doctor. She had to carry him all the way, about a mile. Even though he's only three he must have been heavy. The doctor sent him straight to the isolation ward at Wollongong hospital.

It's Tuesday today as well. Mum said Dad was driving to work in his truck this morning when he felt sick and weak. So he went to the doctor's surgery instead. By the time the ambulance took him to the hospital, he could hardly walk or even sit up. It sounds like he's really bad. Oh, why didn't they have the vaccine like we did? They wouldn't have got this awful disease. Me and Peter and Pauline and Sheelagh walked from school down to the Council Chambers to get the needles. Salk vaccine it's called.

We had our needles before people started to get polio around here. But for the last couple of months, polio has been everywhere, all along the Illawarra Coast. It's been really scary. They call it an epidemic – that's when lots of people get it. Some people have even died. Now Dad has it as well as David, and we don't know what will happen, or whether they'll get better. Mum didn't have the needles. I hope she doesn't catch it. I begin another decade of the Rosary. Peter pokes his head through the door and sees me kneeling there.

'What are you doing?' he says.

'Saying the Rosary for Dad. Want to say it with me?'

'Nah,' he says. 'I'm hungry. Where's the tin of jam?'

I sigh and make the sign of the cross, putting my rosary beads away in a little bag. I'm hungry too, though I hadn't noticed it until that moment. I stood and went into the kitchen.

'I'll cut the bread,' I say, picking up the knife. 'I cut it straighter than you.'

(Girl praying – Linda Brooks)

as kids / Newcastle 1950's - Jo Tregellis

as kids

we saw them

spouting

and thought them

to be far away

we acknowledged them

and went on with our swimming

now...the whales are very close

as kids

we surfed with porpoises

in the swollen green waves

and thought them

to be too close

we admired them

attempted their technique

now...the porpoises are named dolphins

as kids

we romped in the sandhills

boys and girls

whose salty wet lips

discovered juvenile kissing

and touching of body parts

our goosebumps quivered

now...the sandhills are gone

as kids
we fished from
great splintered wood wharves
riveted with rusted steel bolts
our lines wound around jam jars
our dreams shattered by ugly catfish
and water rats the size of dingoes
now...apartments are built over the rats

'I'm going to teach you jolly kids some manners if it kills me!' Mum announced.

It was a wintery Sunday evening. My brother and I exchanged sideways glances and smothered the urge to snicker. Mum hated snickering. She always felt she was the target, regardless of the real cause. Thinking that perhaps we'd been banging the cutlery onto the table a little noisily, I quietened my efforts. My desire to please was not shared by my brother, who increased the decibels accordingly.

I had to admit that for just the four of us we were quite a noisy bunch at mealtimes. Although Mum was fond of domestic order in the house, I had never heard the phrase, 'children should be seen and not heard' at home. Apparently she had developed a repugnance for the phrase in her own childhood and vowed never to use it on her own offspring. When I remembered that she was partial to joining in our lively debates and conversations over the dinner table, I wondered what she had in mind.

'You've got no idea, the pair of you!' Mum said, thumping the casserole onto the table.

Peter snorted. I snickered.

'You needn't think any of that tommyrot will get either of you anywhere!'

Pretending I needed to rush to the dunny, I exploded with laughter.

Mum's direct approach with people was legendary. She was the manager of a grocery store. In my opinion her dealings with customers fell way outside the category of good manners. This was even more evident with Sales Reps. Mum regarded 'reps' on a par with muddy boots—you couldn't help having them, but the less you had to look at them, the better.

Quite frankly, I found her attitude entertaining. More often than not, I was secretly proud of her forthright style, although I would rather have been invisible at times. I used to visit her at work after school, tidying and sorting or weighing vegetables; making sure I was useful. Mum couldn't 'abide' idleness.

I remember one afternoon when one of the haberdashery reps arrived, the aroma of Old Spice preceding him. This alone was enough to displease my mother. Although she held a high standard in personal hygiene, and didn't mind a dash of manly aftershave, she had no time for anyone who 'doused themselves in the stuff'. With a flamboyant swagger the rep sailed towards my mother. The staff, who knew my mother better than he, parted to allow him through. Mum's eyes narrowed as she took in his slicked back hair.

'I told you not to come back for three months,' she stated loudly.

'Oh,' he ventured, undeterred, 'I was in the area and...'

'Nonsense. There aren't any other stores with haberdashery departments within 50 miles. You're just wasting my time.'

'Surely, it must be nearly three months,' he continued, now struggling for ground, with an ever growing audience.

'Five weeks. That's how long it's been. Don't you keep a diary?'

So I couldn't help but feel that Mum's proposal to teach us manners was doomed to failure. I remembered the countless times she had yelled, 'What do you want?' out the kitchen window to visitors. In her book, 'it was ignorant to come sneaking around to the back door'.

My father's amusement was also aroused by Mum's plan. She conveyed it to him when he arrived home from work. However, unlike 'we jolly kids', Dad held his peace. The wicked twinkle in his eye was entirely missed by Mum.

'How are you going to achieve that Else?' he asked reasonably.

'What do you mean 'how am *I* going to achieve it'? A person could do with a bit of help, Max. At the rate those two are going they'll be no better than heathens.'

'Well, of course Else—only too happy to help. What did you have in mind?'

'Meals for a start. They talk over the top of each other. When they're not elbowing each other, they're putting their elbows on the table. If a person was expecting a 'please', they'd die waiting. And this grabbing salt and bread across each other is enough to curl your toes.'

So the lessons began. As all good teachers do, Mum outlined the rules, which might as well be stated at the 'get go'. Dad cheerfully offered to write them down and earned a look of scorn. He was showing far too much enjoyment in an idea that was 'serious business'.

Peter and I slouched in our chairs. 'Slouching' was instantly added to the rules.

'Oh, for crying out loud, Mum,' said Peter. 'Grumbling to the cook' who'd slaved over a hot stove was added swiftly.

'That's a lot to remember Else. You don't think we should start simply?' questioned Dad, justly fearing the list was getting out of control.

'They should have been doing all this for years.' Mum ground out the words. 'A person can only take so much ingratitude and bad manners.'

Being a games addict, Mum decided there should be some form of scoring. A reward for the winner. Dad's eyes grew round.

'Don't overdo it Else.'

'A person gets sick of being accused of overdoing things when other people do nothing. A Freddo frog for the winner won't be 'overdoing' it.'

So the game was on. Dad brought out the peg basket for 'keeping score'. We all started with 10 pegs. Any infraction meant you lost a peg to the person who noticed your misdemeanour. Dad's face glowed. Even Peter and I were infected a sense of excitement. Never had dinner time been such fun. The room was filled with gleeful cries, 'elbows on the table', 'forgot to say please', 'didn't ask to pass the salt', 'he slouched', 'she used the wrong knife', and so on. Even before tea was half way through Mum noticed a disturbing phenomenon. All the pegs were in front of Dad's plate. Mum's had been the first to disappear, at an alarming rate.

'Harrumph,' she muttered.

Undeterred, she soldiered on. Night after night, we watched each other with eagle eyes. Mum concentrated so hard she got a headache. And still she was the first to lose her pegs—over and over again. Never one to give up, she put more effort into it.

'I'm not one for throwing in the towel.'

'Good on you, Else. The kids are learning fast.'

Mum surveyed Dad's face for signs of sarcasm, and finding none, she reluctantly conceded he was right. The glaring fact that she was the worst offender was not voiced. She was taking her failure with considerable grace and we kids were having far too much fun to have it end too soon. Dad's quick hand, and quiet 'you forgot' this or that, had us all on our toes. Although Mum hated to lose or be the butt of any jokes she would not give in. Then one evening we arrived home to find dinner on the table, but no pile of pegs. Our disappointment was palpable.

'Geez, Mum. Where are the pegs?' asked Peter, forgetting for the moment that 'geez' meant the forfeit of two pegs.

'I had a big wash,' said Mum, with a voice of finality. We were gobsmacked. Mum never had washing left on the line in the evening. She even came home from work at lunchtime to take it in.

'Oh well. Who cares,' said Peter. 'Dad won all the Freddos.'

Looking Back; Looking forward - Louise Berry

I look out the window

containers graffitied
by the unruly

wonder what
archaeologists of the future
will say when they discover
remains of our society

will the Time Team
get excited enthuse
over what is revealed

will it see us as
an advanced civilization

or shall we be classed
as primitive
a society without restraint
which shuns its own
respects no one - no thing

I look at the boxes
stacked on top of each other
that some call home

no carvings for the future
inhabitants to hold in awe
wonder at their beauty

I giggle

how we deceive
ourselves and others
with our cost sensitive
ideas of beauty
our lack of respect
for ourselves and others

I close my eyes

'Get out of the road, ya nong!' The man was cranky because he had driven all the way up this road and couldn't find a parking space, now here was this kid standing in the road where there was a vacant spot.

The young man went up to the driver, 'I'm sorry sir, but you will have to move on.'

'Why? I want to park here; me mate lives up the road.'

'I'm sorry sir, but I have been asked to keep this spot free. A wedding car is expected soon.'

'A weddin'? Here? Is this a church or something?'

The young man nodded.

'Oh I see, so that's why yer all ponced up, is it? Flash tie and everythin'. Ah well, good luck,' the man said good-naturedly and drove away. Fifty yards up the road he came across one small parking space and eased the car in.

The young man returned to his post, standing in the road.

It was to be a quiet wedding. The bride, although usually quite shy, had for once, managed to get her own way with her mother. The little timber church in the Sydney suburb, small though it was, provided more than enough seating for the number of invited guests.

This would be almost the last event to be held here; most of the parishioners had already started to worship at the newly built church in the next suburb. This one, on the last block of land available, had been sold to a developer. Large blocks of units had previously appeared, almost overnight, so that now there was barely enough room to park cars in the street.

Michael, the bride's eighteen year old brother, had been given the task of keeping enough space for the bridal car. He was hoping one of his classmates would come by; he had endured more than enough embarrassing moments throughout his school years. Now he was glad all that was behind him and he was looking forward to being employed by his father for a couple of years at least, just while he made up his mind what he would do with his life.

Not that he liked the smell of leather particularly; but he and his sister Marian had enjoyed helping to choose the designs for wallets and handbags on the days their father had invited them along to his factory. Of course his father was delighted that his son had decided to become part of his cherished business and was looking forward to 'showing him the ropes'. It made up for the time he had argued with his daughter, Marian about her lack of interest in the business. Of course it was really Dad's fault he never really understood his only daughter. Come to that, how much did he understand either of his kids. He seldom showed up at school events. Even when Marian had won that small prize it was left to Mum to congratulate her.

And now, Marian was grown-up and about to be married. Not that he was keen on the fella but it was Marian's choice.

Inside the little church, Denise Dixon, the bride's mother, was feeling uncomfortable perched on the end of the front pew. She looked around and saw the girls had done their best yesterday to hide the shabbiness of the place by tying bows of pink ribbons on the ends of the pews. But even with a large bowl of flowers on the platform it still looked what it was, an old chapel built in the early 1920's.

If her husband Ed had been sitting beside her right now, she would point out to him all the inadequacies. She should have insisted on the ceremony being held in the newly built church with its lovely modern stained glass window. Mr and Mrs Brandt might think that their new daughter-in-law came from some common, second-class family. Thank goodness the reception would be up-market in that elegant hotel with no expense being spared there. Sometimes Marian could be so stupid. She had gone along with her father's idea to have the wedding here; but just because both kids had been christened in the place was no reason they had to be married here too!

Denise shifted herself around a bit. This powder blue polyester suit is not proving to be as comfortable as I thought it would be, hopefully it will not show creases; I've been sitting here too long already and the afternoon is warm. But I thought the straight skirt would make me look slim, perhaps I should have worn the cotton blouse underneath instead of the long-sleeved silk one. Ah well, I'll just have to grin and bear it.

How is Marian going to cope with married life? She is such a shy girl, what does she know about the 'facts of life'? I know they are taught these things in school, but I suppose I should have had a mother to daughter talk with her. Too late now, she'll be arriving soon. Where is the organist? Shouldn't she be here to play until the bride arrives and walks down to the strains of the wedding march on her father's arm? Not that it will take very long in this tiny place, hardly enough time to show off that expensive oyster satin gown.

I hope my daughter will be happy; she is so young, she has not yet learned to stand up for what she wants. Not that she ever did, she was always quiet and Ed has always been able to sway the family in the direction he chooses. How is she going to cope with having children? She is so modest, not a bit like the girls with whom she used to knock around. They are all away somewhere else now. Not many of them properly married either. Only that plump girl, Kitty, available to be bridesmaid and she doesn't look all that good in the pink satin dress she has chosen for the occasion. And the bouquets only just arrived in the nick of time. It's taken three phone calls to the florist to get them. And what's more this orchid pinned to my suit is the wrong colour. It is to be hoped that Mrs Brandt has no colour sense. She may not notice things like that.

The door at the back of the platform opened and Ivor, the bridegroom, and his best man came through to stand at the front. Ivor cast an eye around, noting how many people and yet how few of his own friends were there. Then he looked anxiously at the front pew where his parents should have been sitting. He said a few words to Bob his best mate. Bob went down the aisle to the entrance and stood looking out. Ivor perched himself on the edge of the pew beside his new mother-in-law. Denise had to shift along to accommodate him. 'I don't know why my folks are so late,' he said.

Denise smiled rather weakly, and thought of patting his hand in case he was nervous but refrained from doing so. 'No doubt the traffic is bad today. Football matches and so on,' she said, 'Don't worry, I'm sure they are on their way. They'll be here in time, you'll see.'

Looking at him closely, Denise thought, I can't think what Marian sees in this young man. He is neatly dressed today, of course, a bit different to his usual garb. His dark eyes are quite penetrating when he looks at you. He is tall enough and broad shouldered, but I don't know - there is something about him; I can't quite take to him really. Still, he is her choice, Mother's opinions don't count when their daughters choose a mate, not these days in Australia anyway. My grandchildren could be quite good-looking, I suppose. It will be nice having little children around again.

Ivor's smile in return was even weaker than hers. Denise is not my choice as a mother-in-law. Her appearance today is quite outrageous, over-made-up and that stupid hat. Not a woman I can like, but then, fortunately, I'm not marrying the mother. And father does have a thriving business of his own. Better to be charming to them both. We don't know if my job will be ongoing, they are making people redundant every week. Ed should offer me a good job in his factory, overseer or something. Who knows, he might even think of me as management material, if I play my cards right.

Denise shifted again. I don't much like the idea of that flat above a take-away shop on a main road, but it's a start for them. Perhaps later I can persuade Ed to help them towards a proper home; when the children start to arrive. Thank goodness we do not have to see too much of the senior Brandt's, not our kind of people really. No doubt we shall have to visit at Christmas, but it is a long drive to Adelaide. They'll expect to see something of their grandchildren of course. Pity Marian didn't choose someone whose family lived in the same state at least.

Suddenly the best man came back from where he had been peering up the street, looking out for a stray taxi. He was followed by Mr and Mrs Brandt. They were both hot and flustered.

'Stupid taxi took us to the wrong church,' Mr Brandt said in a loud voice tinged with a slight accent. 'He said he thought this one was pulled down last year. Looks like it should have been.'

Mrs Dixon stiffened as he looked around at the tiny windows, the walls with paint peeling and the cobwebs hanging from the ceiling.

Ivor stood up to give his mother a peck on the cheek and did his best to calm the situation. 'Now Dad, don't be like that. You're here now. Say hello to Mrs Dixon.' Mrs Brandt caught her breath at last and seated herself in the opposite pew after nodding to Denise. Ivor sat with her and gradually she calmed down. She was wishing her son had stayed in South Australia.

He could have found a bride there. Even better if he'd waited until his second cousin Gerda had arrived from Europe. She might have been more suitable as a wife. He is our only son after all and we don't see much of him. Gerda is just about the right age for him. I think she speaks English; anyway it will not take her too long to learn. European girls are so clever. I hope Gerda stays for a long time and gets to know Ivor.

It's all been too much; the flight from Adelaide; followed by the bus from the airport to the suburbs; and to top it off having to meet with this awful, snobbish family; not to mention this silly young girl my son is marrying! With his looks he should be marrying a model, at least!

I'm not keen on the motel they booked either. The bed is too small for us. I didn't sleep at all well last night. My first trip to Sydney is not as pleasant as I had hoped it would be. I don't know why people want to live in such a big city. Such a noisy sort of place with all that traffic, I'm glad I don't have to live here. Give me the country, even if we do have to work long hours.

I was hoping to find Mrs Dixon to be a likeable sort of person, someone I can talk to. But just look at her! How could anybody think of wearing a hat like that? It's true it matches her suit, but it is a large, overbearing sort of thing. And who was it that chose orchids for the mothers to wear. I hate orchids. It couldn't have been Ivor. Ivor has more taste than that.

I wish he'd never thought of coming to this city. Even Melbourne was closer than Sydney. Just think that I've got to keep coming here, just to see the grandchildren. I must persuade him to move back at some time or other; we could find them a nice little cottage near us. I've always hoped Ivor would move back. Five years is too long to be away from one's family. Why would he want to take a job like a fork-lift driver? He would be much better following his father's trade. Stephan could have helped him so much. It almost broke my heart when Ivor left so suddenly. Mrs Brandt fished in her handbag for a tiny handkerchief to dab at the corner of her eye. When is this wedding going to get started? Don't tell me the bride is going to be late! I wouldn't care if she doesn't turn up at all.

A plump woman came through the door in the centre of the platform and took her place at the side, she was just as out-of-breath and disturbed as Mrs Brandt had been. She started playing softly, something of Beethoven's on the small organ. It was just recognisable enough for Stephan Brandt to perk himself up and think, that's more like it, something distinguished at last. You can't beat a good German composer like Beethoven.

The organist changed the tune and then nodded to Ivor who took the hint and stood up, back rigid, facing the bowl of flowers. Bob, his best man stood beside him, but by contrast he was relaxed, almost sloppy in his bearing.

There was a hum of excitement from the back. The bride was arriving! All heads turned in that direction. Out of the gloom stepped Ed Dixon with his daughter Marian hanging on to his arm. They progressed slowly down the aisle to Wagner's Bridal Music from Lohengrin. The organist had played it many times before, but still it did not have the grand sound it deserved.

But nobody really noticed this omission as they were more interested in the overall picture - what the bride was wearing, what her hairstyle was like and what flowers she was carrying. Marian walked steadily, aware that all eyes were on her, but she was glad to have her father's arm to hold.

Mrs Dixon had her head tilted to one side as a slow tear tried to ooze from her eye.

Mrs Brandt stood with her back like a ramrod, doing her best not to smile.

Mr Brandt nodded his head once. She really is a pretty little thing; perhaps my son made a good choice after all. She looks bed-worthy. I noticed the other day she has good legs. Good strong legs to wrap around a man, to hold him close! He shivered slightly and licked his lips.

Ivor tried to relax. If only men did not have to go through all this to get a girl. But I know I would never have persuaded Marian to shack up with me. Not in a million years, not this girl! Ivor turned towards Marian as she arrived by his side. He lifted her veil to drape it back over the tiara and her long titian hair.

God! She does look beautiful! I'm very glad we met that day on the bus. I was so surprised when she didn't mind me sitting beside her; there were plenty of vacant seats. She is very reticent but somehow I like that. I look forward to showing her how!

Marian thought, I hope I don't do anything wrong, it all seems so overwhelming, such a lot of ceremony, but it will keep mother happy. But this is only half-way through. Why did I have to have some silly person to do my make-up? I'm quite capable of doing my own. All mum's idea of course. I should have suggested to Ivor that we elope and save all this bother. One's wedding day is supposed to be so special and that's not at all how I feel. I just feel nervous. But I know Mum would have been very disappointed if we had eloped.

I can hardly believe Ivor proposed, I never thought he would; or that I would say yes. Still, I am really looking forward to going to Surfers tomorrow for two weeks and then coming back to my own little home.

Kitty, the only bridesmaid, walked behind Marian trying not to trip in her new high heels. Isn't this exciting? I never expected I'd be asked to be bridesmaid. Everybody I know has been a bridesmaid several times but this is my first! That best man is rather nice; I hope I made a good impression on him when we met on Thursday. His name is Bob. That's a nice name, I hope he likes me. I wonder if he can dance, it would be a pity if after all those dancing lessons I took I don't get asked to dance. But the best man is supposed to dance with the bridesmaid isn't he? Or is it the bridegroom? Oh dear, I wish I knew about weddings and what one is expected to do. I know the bride is supposed to throw her bouquet and whoever catches it is the one who is next to get married. I really must try to catch it when Marian throws it. Doesn't Marian look lovely, I wish I had her figure. What do I do now? When do I take the bouquet from Marian?

The minister smiled encouragingly at Marian and Ivor, before starting solemnly on the formal rites. The ceremony proceeded without any mishaps, the best man had not lost the ring; Ivor said his vows properly and in a clear voice; Marian made her responses and vows in her usual soft voice; and Kitty managed to hold the two bouquets without dropping them.

The register was signed as the organist played 'Love Me Tender'. Another decision made by Mrs Dixon, who was an Elvis Presley fan, even though Marian had suggested they play a record of something by Roy Orbison. Ivor had many of the singer's recordings; Marian had spent many an evening listening to them.

They proceeded back down the aisle to the strains of the Wedding March but it was almost unrecognisable. The organist had hoped to convey a triumphal sound but the old organ wasn't up to it. However it was loud enough because nobody heard the first patter of raindrops on the tin roof. The newly wedded couple emerged to find the photographer standing under a large umbrella in the pouring rain. All the wedding guests crowded and jostled under the tiny porch behind the bridal couple, almost tipping them onto the grass.

The photographer suggested he take only one picture because of the weather. But he would take as many as they wished at the reception. He had already reconnoitred and decided on the most opportune sites in the hotel for pictures that would be favourable to his budding business and he hoped his new camera would prove to be a good one.

Nobody could complain things didn't go well. No-one was more pleased about this than Denise Dixon. She sighed. Hopefully the reception would proceed without a hitch. She had heard of many a fine wedding being followed by disastrous events at the reception. This would not happen to anything Denise Dixon had arranged......

To be continued...(see 'Unravelling')

When I was a boy living in my home town of Newcastle, NSW, my constant companion was a Labrador Retriever named Caesar. In the 1970s all dogs seemed to have been named after kings, like Caesar, Kaiser, Rex, or... King. He arrived as an 8 month old youngster on our doorstep when we lived in Ipswich Queensland. I was about five at the time. Caesar had belonged to another family and they gave him to us. I believe it was because they lived somewhere where they weren't allowed to have pets. My dad was in the Air Force and in 1974 he was transferred to Newcastle, and our dog came with us.

Caesar was walked every day by my father and, when I was old enough to go to the park by myself, around the age of 9, I would take Caesar with me, let him off the leash when we arrived at the park, then tie him up again and walk him home where he always hurriedly slurped down a dog dish full of water.

Most of the time he was kept in our large back yard. My parents were scared if they let him roam the streets he might end up in the local pound or run over on the road. He seemed content with this for the first few years until he found out he could escape over the fence at night, wander around the local bushland for hours on end, and return in the early hours of the morning. No-one would have been the wiser, had he not reeked to high heaven of the tossed garbage bags he'd nuzzle through, and sported a tide mark along his belly showing he'd been swimming in ponds, no doubt trying and failing to get his paws on local wildlife (more on that practice later).

During the day Caesar would laze around like other dogs, occasionally going for a drink of water around the back of the house, or sitting in the sun while my mum would hang out the clothes on the 1950's style fence-to-fence clothesline. Then, at about 3:00pm every day he'd instinctively get up and make his way either over the fence, or if it was open, through one of the side gates and up the street where he'd sit on the footpath, looking down the hill waiting for the school bus that would carry my younger brother, sister and myself home.

Then, after the bus would depart, he'd stand and stare at the vaguely recognizable children in the distance, waiting for us to get closer. Then we'd call out his name and he'd come running, his ham tongue dripping saliva down those black rubber-like gums to the tar road. We'd greet him, pat his head and he'd accompany us home where we'd get afternoon sandwiches and cordial from Mum, and watch TV.

Occasionally, just to gently tease him, we'd get off the bus at the next stop, creep around the corner, wait until he was watching the other way, and make it to our front fence by hiding behind nature strip trees. He'd be confused that we hadn't jumped off the bus, but then he'd be relieved when we called out his name. The race up the stairs to the front door was always a close one with one happy Labrador right on our tails.

Back in Queensland, Caesar had been a bit of a handful, although one had to see the humour in the predicaments he found himself in. Once, he disappeared for a day until my dad received a phone call, asking if he owned a golden Labrador. My dad said yes, and then jumped in the car to go pick up this juvenile delinquent who had met up with a more experienced black Labrador earlier that day and decided to chase some chickens. Dad found Caesar tied up, feeling very sorry for himself. The man who called said the other dog was probably the ringleader, and Caesar the gullible sidekick.

Then, there was fun with my mother driving the family car. One day she was learning to drive - and this was about 1973 - with the driving school instructor sitting in the passenger seat and as she drove the streets of Eastern Heights, Ipswich, she happened to glance in her rear vision mirror to see a very tired looking dog running behind her. She pulled over to the side of the road and saw, to her alarm, our dog's paws worn down so much they were bleeding. The car wasn't hers and she thought our dog would make a mess on the back seat, so she turned the car around and drove slowly back, allowing Caesar a leisurely hobble back home to where his feet were treated with something soothing like Rawleigh's 'Antiseptic Salve' or lanolin.

When we moved to Newcastle in 1974 my mum didn't often drive, but one day Caesar saw her driving a few streets away from home. He thought he'd surprise her by jumping through the driver's door window right onto her lap! Trouble was the car wasn't ours, and the woman wasn't my mother. Our dog had a puzzled look on his face as the woman quite understandably screamed in panic.

When I was about 13 I used to walk over to the local shopping centre a mate of mine, Bill. We didn't have much money in those days, usually enough for a drink, some chips or a few cinnamon donuts, but we liked to go the record shop, called The Green Apple, and also to look at bikes at Norman Ross. Getting away from the house without Caesar seeing us and following was a difficult one; even my mother if she went out in the day on errands, would be quiet when she shut and locked the front door as our loyal dog would hear her, start whimpering, then bound over the fence and 'walk her' down to the bus stop. One day he followed my brother and I down to the bus stop and jumped right on the bus with us, much to the amusement of the other kids on the bus.

He was ordered off by me, the door shut and the bus took off, the dog running for a 100 metres or so before he tired and the bus was out of sight.

One Thursday night, the traditional late shopping night, Bill and I grabbed around $5.00 each and trotted off to Garden City. Two streets away from home, I could hear a dog's feet padding the road, and panting. You guessed it, Caesar had decided we needed company. I was afraid he would get run over so I ordered him home. I'd point homeward, yell: 'No! Go home!' He'd look in the direction of the finger, look back to smile and then pant. No matter what I did he wouldn't listen. So he came with us.

In a moment of impetuous foolishness I decided to split from him when we arrived at Garden City. I thought he'd just stay out the front on the grass and we could gather him on our way home a couple of hours later. I told him to stay. He didn't. I told him to go home. He wouldn't. He just followed us into the centre like he was our brother. So, there we were, two 13 year old boys and a Labrador walking through Garden City Kotara with everyone staring at us. (It was so embarrassing for me at that fragile age.) We walked into the David Jones store. It was there that we finally lost Caesar when we jumped on the Up escalator. Caesar had never seen moving stairs and just stood looking up at me as I disappeared.

Bill and I went around the top floor and took our time looking at stereos, watching TV, checking out sports equipment, and generally having a good time. We were away maybe 20 minutes and then we rode the down escalator when we soon heard loud, mournful howling. It was Caesar, at the base of the escalator, still waiting for me and surrounding him were three or four very attractive David Jones' girls, trying to console my dog. Before I could escape, Caesar turned his head and when he saw me he bounded towards me and when I stepped off the escalator he jumped up in excitement.

The David Jones' girls there were very cross with us, abandoning the dog like we did. One said to me: 'Is this your dog?' I nodded. 'Well, you should be ashamed leaving him like this. He's been very worried!'

Red faced, we left the shopping centre. Personally, I was very annoyed Caesar had 'caused so much trouble,' but my dog didn't care as he had his owner back, he felt safe and his adventure was finally over.

Three Cheeky Monkeys - Christina Batey

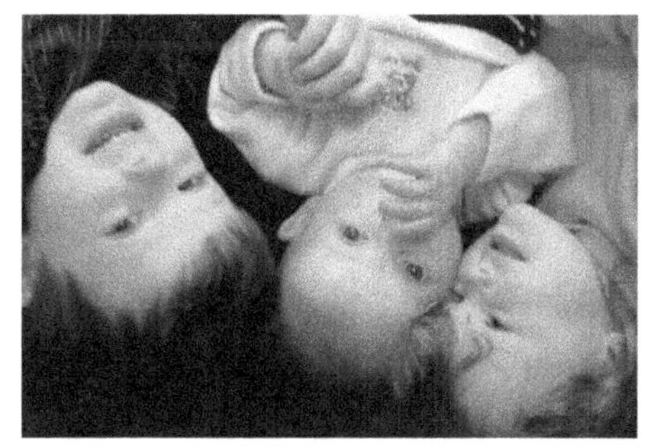

Three little grins
shining like the sun
three cheeky Monkeys
see none, hear none, speak none

Three constant voices
they laugh, they sing, they talk
three little pairs of legs
That ran before they walked

Three little cyclones
tearing through the house
Now what are they up to?
they're quiet as a mouse

Three dirty pairs of hands
dextrously unfurled
three tiny treasures
the most precious in the world

(Family photo – author)

Today is the day Les came to fix my piano.

Well, not completely 'fix', mind you. The whole procedure is more like starting off with a little section first and following the procedures until it's better. Taking off the 115 year old, little cast iron wheels and replacing them with - 'you beaut - super duper', German engineered, double silicon, overhead cam, 2008 wheels, which come with a 'satisfaction guarantee of quality', was a classic place to start. That's step one.

Step two - Les has taken away the guts. He will replace the graphite whirligigs—I have no idea what he called them. Then, he informs me, he'll replace the mottled, whalebone keyboard with modern materials, preferably something that was never alive, he did tell me, but I can't remember what. I think nylon had a lot to do with the outcome. As I looked at the now redundant keys, I thought they looked uncannily like the teeth on an eighty year old man, with even the odd one missing here and there.

Step three - he'll bring all the related bits and pieces back from the dead by polishing any rust and built up dirt away, put them inside the veneered, walnut shell of my piano, clean the wires and tune it.

Easy, no problem, Les's family have been piano tuners and fixers for generations. He is actually a fifth generation piano man, that's quite an amazing profession really. Not too many people can say they come from a family that has been doing the same job for nearly 200 years.

While Les was operating inside the body of my sick instrument he came across two little, silver threepenny bits that he handed to me. Holding these tiny coins in my hand, I cast my mind back to what Les had told me about the history of the Hapsburg. These pianos where brought out to Australia in their hundreds during the late 19th century and early 20th century. You still see them in country halls, scout halls, churches and the like—not to mention the odd life-saving club.

They were favoured here because of their iron frame. Apparently, the pianos from England had wooden frames and would twist and warp in the hot and dry Aussie climes—or if you were in the top end, hot and wet Aussie climes. It seemed that no matter which part of the country you lived in, wooden-framed pianos just didn't cut it out here, and so they went the way of the dinosaur, superseded by their more robust cousins.

I'm starting to sound a bit like David Attenborough on the *Life of Mammals*. No matter. Where was I? Ah yes, the life of the Hapsburg piano! So the iron-framed piano was quite a boon to have in your drawing room, or 'the front room' as it was referred to by my Nan, who also told us in no uncertain tone to 'stay out!'

Families would gather at the end of the working day and sit and sing along to the sounds of the tunes that were belted out across the country. Whole generations of Aussie 'clubbies' would dance and sing to the tunes filtering out of halls on a hot summer Saturday night out. Of course, the songs that rang out, in suburbia and the city, depended on the era of the time.

'Click Goes the Shears', *'Ryebuck Shearer'* and *'Molly Malone'* would have been jolly good tunes to sing to during colonial days. However, I guess the wars, both the first and second, brought on a variety of ditties like *'It's a Long Way to Tipperary'*, and *'Pack up Your Troubles'*. These were popular in drawing rooms across the land. There was a little tin on top of 'The Beasty' and people would feed their threepenny bits into it. This may have been a weekly allowance to gather enough coins to pay for the piano. Many a time, mothers would have to sell their favourite piece of furniture to pay the rent, perhaps losing the only source of music available to the family.

To say my piano is old is a bit of an understatement really. It was built before the invention of the motor car, it's been through two world wars, and lived through the time men landed on the moon. It was around when the telephone become an everyday item in the family home, and television and computers replaced it as the main source of entertainment for families.

I don't know all the adventures my particular piano has been through. I know it has survived my Uncle's kids, who now have kids of their own, and it has lived through the traumas of belonging to my sister's boys. Her eldest boy is now nearly 21 years old and has up-graded to a more modern, concert pitched instrument, which would blow the doors off mine, if indeed they were to compete. My own kids learnt on it, but as to its other seventy or eighty years of history, she hides her secrets well.

The two threepenny bits we found inside her are dated 1951 and 1958. Perhaps the owners were six-pence short of the payment, and had to sell her. The rest, as they say, is history.

Hopefully, Les will bring her back to life and I shall call her my 'Lazarus piano'. Maybe I'll even learn how to play -it would be a shame to just let her fall into disrepair again, after 115 years. I couldn't bear the thought of the old girl ending her life at the local tip, like so many that have gone before.

Sunrise from Dad's Window - Linda Visman

On the distant morning shore,
a globe of bright orange ascends,
cut into strips by ribbons of cloud.
Gold light catches on the lake,
a second sun, rippling.

The wakening beams stream along
a narrow, straight-edged corridor.
Within those confining walls,
they stretch closer and closer
towards where I stand at the window.

Grey ripples exchange drabness for gold,
and the glittering patch of water on my side
becomes one with the brilliant pathway
that links the lake from side to side.

My eyes are dazzled but I cannot leave.
I watch as the sun comes into full glory,
As it does, the lighted corridor withdraws,
retreats into its brilliant source.
In a moment it is gone, and I feel bereft.

Then the gold is replaced by silver,
a glow that suffuses the still waters
with softness and warmth.
No longer confined to the narrow corridor,
it spreads across the whole lake.

I turn away, back into my father's home,
and prepare for another day by his side.
I have a gift to take to the hospital for him -
another sunrise.

Adam was born in 1972 with a severe disability. Diagnosed at an early age with Tuberous Sclerosis Complex and given a minimal chance of leading a 'normal' life or living past his teens by a medical specialist, he defied this early prognosis. He has had to face prejudice and fight for equal rights in areas that most of us take for granted.

His local community were generally supportive and embraced Adam and his family's needs. They often gave Adam and his family support and encouragement when the going got tough.

Adam lives is a small township in the Dandenong Ranges in Victoria and was included in all community activities from a young age, such as get-togethers with the towns Country Fire Brigade, Primary School, cubs and scouts and family dances in the local community hall.

This community consisted of many individuals who gave support when it was needed most. Through these stories it is intended to touch on some of the people and events that shaped Adam's life.

Adam's journey began when his disability was diagnosed, travelling to a centre for up to two hours each way in a bus every day away from home and making it back, through an integration program at his local school.

He was given a voice through facilitated communication, which enabled him to express personal thoughts with poetry. The stories continue through to 2009 where Adam's personal ongoing plan has been developed and included in a request for support from the Department of Human Services. An ongoing discussion with bureaucracy that seems never ending.

Adam's impact on people and their attitudes in the community has been more than an awareness of disability. He challenged people's thinking about how the system supports an individual, because he chose to take a different path and attend a regular school.

Thus, several of his teachers re-looked at how they worked with all children, thereby benefiting the whole school community.

Adam has the background of a caring and loving family involved in cultural and individual pursuits that allowed all of our children, and us, all to grow and develop.

When it came to the role of his grandparents, Adam never missed out. His grandmother, Wilma, is an accomplished poet and gave him much encouragement and attention. She loved receiving his poems, many written specifically for Bert and herself.

Some of the poems were serious and some witty and cheeky - as shown in the poem Bertie, written especially for his grandfather.

BERTIE
Slim as a dear rude structure and grandly
defined.
Nicely developed is he.
Ask women what reason they wish
he was theirs
and they answer in chorus together
as one.
Dear Bert is a wonder as things
he can do.
So willing to please to invent and create
dear Granma wishes that
he would grow perhaps
out
and have more to eat
so the fellow won't starve.
But Bert is not fooled
by the wonder of food
which slows ill the mind
from creating
and more.
He looks fine to me
and he'll go for a while yet.

Adam 1988

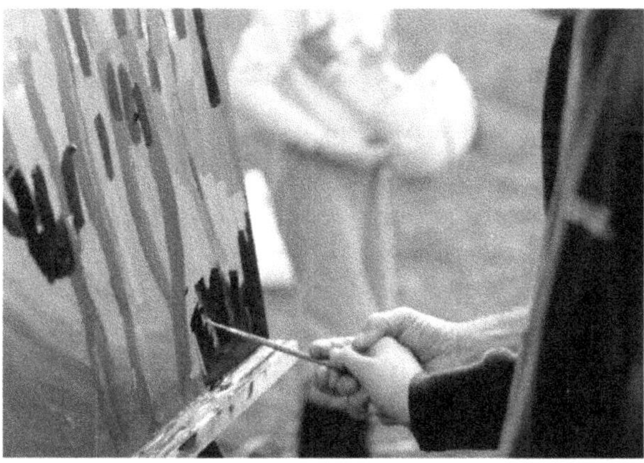

On family holidays, I often took along paint, brushes and other stuff so our children Tevi, Amy, Joel and I could complete the odd masterpiece. Adam had taken a lesser role in these early holiday activities prior to his visit to Rosemary.

On one of our holidays where we stayed in a lovely farmhouse in Northern Victoria, 'Adam as Artist' began to evolve. A pine plantation surrounded the area and Adam had written a powerful piece of poetry describing the destruction of our natural forest with this introduced species. It described in detail, rotting timber, strangled forests, no undergrowth and ants feeding on the waste below. Great visual material for any artist looking for inspiration. The following poem by Adam inspired the painting below, which was painted by Adam also.

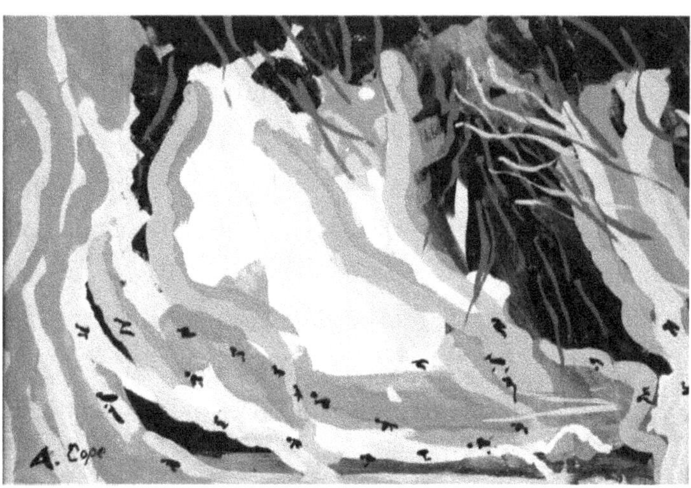

'Yellow light streams through the quiet glade
and washes over the loneliness.
Slithering westerly saying nothing and giving
not a sound.
Death slowly moving across the ground.'

After dinner I sat with Adam and the other children as they prepared to paint. As they were painting Adam completed his poem with my assistance on his communication board and he asked if he could paint as well. During the conversation on subject matter I suggested he might like to use his poem as a reference to which he agreed.

As an art teacher when working with students I give them some basic rules to work to: Block in the background first with the main colour or colours then build over this background the other parts of the intended painting. Use larger brushes when you need to paint a large area quickly and smaller ones for fine detail. Mix the paint smoothly so it flows easily from the brush to paper. Ensure the brush is loaded with paint before you begin. Preferably apply lighter colours first followed by darker ones over the top and avoid where possible direct black in the early stages of a painting.

Using these rules and his poem I phrased questions for Adams response: What colour do you wish to use in the background? Do you want the colour to be light or dark? Do you want the colour to be warm or cool? Is it okay if I mix it for you first and you can let me know when it's correct? Show me with your hand where you want to place the trees. (Offer hand support and allow him to indicate where on the board he wants to apply the paint.) Is this colour okay? etc.

It took a long time to work through questions and obtain responses and then to assist him to actually paint. Question – response – check the response has been understood – hands on support with a section of the artwork - mix up a colour – check it's right – further questions – new action and so on. The facilitation required was very firm hand support that enabled Adam to hold the brush effectively, and at the same time actually move it onto and around the board's area. Holding his response back until he was ready was absolutely crucial. Even as he was sweeping the paint down and/or across the canvas, I had to be alert, ready to stop him from any involuntary movement.

Adam does not have the ability to mix paint and apply it independently onto the art board. His cognitive skills were poor due to his apraxia. The entire painting took several hours of communication, chatter and physical support.

This dense struggle - Linda Brooks

This dense struggle,
this dark night
that warred and wrangled with my soul;
is past.

Some wars don't have to be won,
just fought.
For losing is its own victory.
We dared.

We wrenched forth courage
from deep within;
we breathed deep the air of hope,
clung to justice.

When we failed we were still heroes;
though reward caressed our hearts,
and then left,
it gave its beauty to our struggle.

By 1957, we'd been out of the four-berth caravan for over a year. Dad had bought a tiny three-roomed cottage from his boss, and transported it from Dapto. There was only one tiny bedroom, and the four of us kids shared its double bed – I was the third child and slept across the bottom. Our parents used a night-and-day settee in the small lounge room that they had to make up every morning and night. Then Dad built an extra room onto the back of it, a bedroom for us four kids. Mum and Dad could have their own bedroom at last. But only for a short time. Mum's brother and family came from England and moved in with us. Mum and Dad moved back out of the bedroom so Uncle and Aunty could have it. Our two cousins somehow managed to fit in the new bedroom with us. Dad again got busy, building a two-roomed garage next to the house. Its small front room served as a very basic kitchen, the back one as a bedroom, into which Aunty and Uncle moved.

In 1958, our baby brother joined the family and Dad was building again, two more bedrooms. The kitchen (which in 2009 still has its original small cupboards) would remain the same, but the L-shaped house would become a rectangle, with the new rooms filling in the space. It was a year of high rainfall in New South Wales and Dad was often rained off the building projects he worked on for Brooks and Wright Builders. During those down times, Dad worked on our house. He says he did more work on our house in those days than he did on his regular work, even in the rain. When he'd finished the framework, we could walk out of the kitchen door onto the open floor joists. If we wanted to go out the back to the pan toilet, we could go the long way round, across where Dad had laid boards on top of the joists towards the side of the house. Or we could go the shorter way, which involved stepping from joist to joist, to the back frame, then jumping down to the ground. You can guess which way we kids preferred to go and, before long, we were racing across them as if they were a solid floor.

One day, having been cooped up for hours by incessant rain, I was eager to get outside to play. The joists were still wet, but that didn't stop me from skipping across them at top speed on my way to the back yard. I was almost there when my foot slipped off the second-last joist. I couldn't save myself and my legs crashed between the joists. But my momentum carried me forward, and my upper body landed fair on top of the two-inch wide hardwood timber. The air rushed out of my lungs and I was left gasping. I flopped across the joist, staring down at the bits of rubble, scraps of wood and dark wet earth, scared and disoriented, the pain in my chest making it impossible to breathe.

I must have groaned or called out, or Dad heard me when I fell, because suddenly he was there. He asked if I could speak and I dazedly shook my head. He carefully picked me up and carried me inside. By the time he'd placed me on the bed I was breathing again, but my chest hurt. After a quick conference with Mum, Dad took me out to his work truck and we were on our way to the doctor's surgery. Dr Needham didn't think any of my ribs were broken, just badly bruised, but he said I should be strapped up, just in case. I wondered what kind of strap would go around my chest. Was it like a big leather belt? Would I be able to move?

The strapping turned out to be a wide strip of sticking plaster, just like Mum or Dad used to cut from a roll to keep the lint in place when we'd cut or grazed ourselves (there were no Band Aids then). However this plaster was much wider. Dad helped Dr Needham stick it in place right around my skinny chest. It covered me from my armpits to my waist and was very uncomfortable, pulling on my skin whenever I moved – which I tried not to do anyway, because it hurt my ribs.

I had to keep the plaster on for several weeks, and it soon became very grubby. Underneath, my skin became irritated and itched like crazy. I wanted to scratch but couldn't. The edges of the plaster frayed and bits of fabric tickled me as well. How I hated it! My ribs soon felt fine, and I kept asking Dad when it could come off. Finally the day came when Dad could remove that hated plaster. Slowly, inch by inch, he peeled it off. My skin was red and tender, and felt strangely cold without its covering. But at last it was gone and I was very thankful. While I'd been strapped up, Dad worked hard to get the room finished. He got the corrugated iron roof on and the floorboards laid in quick time. Now nobody could slip on those joists again.

With Mum's brother and family in the garage and our cousins sharing our bedroom, my parents had been able to have their own bedroom again. However they didn't get it for long. Dad was still building the extension when Mum's parents arrived from England. Mum and Dad had to give up their room for Grandma and Granddad, and go back to the night-and-day in the lounge room. But when the building was done, we had two more bedrooms.

Granddad, who never helped my parents with a penny the whole time they were with us, gave my uncle money to finance the building of his house. However it was many months before it was completed and they all moved into it, finally leaving just the seven of us to our own place.

For us carefree kids, life was good back then, but when I see the burdens my parents carried – as did many other migrants at that time, I realise how difficult it had been for them.

Parting - Gail Hennessy

(for Mark)

Lying on a mattress in the lounge room
on the morning you are about to leave

you look up at me from your caramel eye
and I enter your eyes and almost drown

you say 'take care of that toe'
(I've lost one already)

I remember your last words at another parting
in Trafalgar Square

'I'll never not miss you'
before you walked away and didn't look back

It is enough.

Mummy! There's cows in our backyard! - Roslyn Jewel

We lived in Naman Street, Dubbo when all the excitement happened. I was five years old that day, my sister Margaret was only two and Vicki was a baby. Dad had built the house himself when Mum was pregnant with me. He was the OIC in charge of Dubbo Airport and worked shift work. He somehow still managed to find enough time to build our house. It was a modest three bedroom fibro house with a tin roof. We had an enclosed back veranda where Margie and I used to play.

Dad had planted out our backyard with a dozen or so fruit trees of different varieties. We had a lemon, orange, mandarin and a few plums and apricots. It provided some much needed shade on a hot summer's day.

One afternoon, Mum put Margie and Vicki down for a nap and told me to just read quietly to myself as she was going to have a sleep too. She used to get very tired with three young children at home and she would have an afternoon nap most days.

While Mum was asleep. I looked through one of my picture books, I heard strange stomping noises in our backyard. I got up on one of the chairs and looked out the window. There was a cow in our backyard. She was a nice black and white cow and was just standing there minding her own business. Suddenly, she was joined by lots of black and white cows. They had all walked down our driveway and were now in our backyard, milling around under the fruit trees. I had never seen cows in our backyard before and I was fascinated. This was much more interesting than looking at a picture book.

They started eating the grass and then they started eating the leaves on our fruit trees. I thought I'd better wake Mummy up. It was never a good idea to wake Mummy up from her nap. I had learned that she never liked to be woken up for anything trivial.

I ran into the bedroom and shook her on the shoulder.

'Mummy, there's cows in our backyard and they're eating our fruit trees.' She blinked at me a few times before I exclaimed, 'There is Mum, lots of black and white cows.'

'What! Cows! Where?'

'In our yard Mummy, eating our fruit trees,' I announced excitedly.

She jumped off the bed and ran out to the back door. She stood there for a few seconds taking it all in.

'You stay inside and don't let your little sister come out either,' she demanded.

I'll never forget the spectacle of our backyard full of black and white cows just munching the leaves off Dad's much-loved fruit trees.

Mummy grabbed the straw broom and marched determinedly down our back steps. She whacked the first cow she came to, soundly on the bottom.

'SHOO! SHOO!' she yelled. 'SHOO! SHOO! GET OUT! GET OUT!'

She showed great bravery, because they were very large cows indeed. It took her quite a while to round them up and head them down the driveway.

She somehow managed to chase them all out of our yard by herself, after which she locked the driveway gates.

'That'll keep them out,' she said smugly.

When dad got home from work, she told him that I'd woken Mum up and told her there was a herd of cows in our yard eating our fruit trees.

'Come outside and I'll show you, Dad.'

He was very surprised to hear the excitement of the day and he carried the baby. Mum, Margie and I followed him down the back steps and out into the yard in procession, to inspect the damage.

'There's not too much damage done, thanks to you,' Dad announced, proudly patting me on the head.

Dad was very happy there were now some very large cow pats in the yard. 'I'll dig them in under the trees. They'll make good fertilizer,' he stated, pleased with himself.

I heard Mum telling dad that the cows must have got out from the dairy up at the end of our road. Someone had probably left the gate open and they must have wandered down the road until they came to the next open gate, which was ours.

After that, when Dad left for work, he always closed the gate after him.

Like Tarzan of the word
you swing metaphors
across the huge gulf
that separates one universe
from another.

Suggestive paradigms
smooth the path
thicket of vines
can't obstruct
your yodelling holler.

Between the part and the whole
leopard skin membrane
tracks the flow
behaviour to attitude
pretence of company
safe enough to
reveal everything
truth hidden
beneath layers of confession.

Where do you go
once your network
of egos, alters, family, colleagues
friends (you don't know)
grows so large, it forms its own
matrix
a series of ties, cliques,
and fleeting collaborations
past internal reference.

How do you do that Tarzan trick
once more
drag the morass
to the moment
that shaky bubble
in which you
misunderstood poet
sit.

Money doesn't grow on trees, you know! - Julie Cochrane

My Dad was a boy during the years of the Great Depression. He witnessed his father working long and hard to support his wife and two children. He watched his mother 'make do' with things when there was no money to buy the necessary resources for life. He learnt to 'be careful' and not waste anything. Little was thrown away. It was kept 'just in case' it could be recycled later - socks with holes in were never thrown away and replaced with new ones, they were darned, and then darned again.

He wore hand-me-downs, and shared a bed with his sister. He walked places because there was no car and it was cheaper than catching a bus. He learnt that neighbours helped one another out and shared what they could. He learnt to appreciate the little things in life and to see a blessing in every circumstance.

My father was determined that the lessons he had learned through the tough days of the Great Depression were passed down to me, and my three siblings. He wisely understood the intrinsic life values that are born out of such hardships and was keen that his four *Baby Boomers* should not miss out on incorporating these treasures into their lives.

My Dad worked hard, and saved hard. We kids never wanted for anything of value. BUT we did it tougher than any other kids I knew! I suffered greatly growing up. I had to wear hand-me-downs from my older sister. I had to dye my white summer Church shoes black instead of buying a new pair for winter. Sometimes Dad would even put new rubbers on the soles of our shoes when holes appeared, rather than buy us *new* shoes. Dad was always 'on our back' about turning lights off, and finishing up every crumb of food on our dinner plates. I lost count of how many times I remained at the tea table gloomily staring down on a plate of cold beans and mashed potato, while the others went off to bed.

It was grossly unfair that Dad would not buy us a TV when every other kid in the street had one. Thankfully our friends Pam Denton and Burnie Boyd allowed us to watch *Superman, Rin Tin Tin* and *Annie Oakley* on their TVs after school each day. We always stayed as long as we could – right up until their Mums put their dinners on the table and suggested we might like to go home and have ours. Fortunately, Mr Chipps from next door, who worked at Grace Brothers, took pity on us and arranged for Dad to hire a TV over the school holidays one year. We had to feed it 2/- every now and then, but we kids thought we were just IT!

For some reason Dad never understood the humiliation he put us through when it came to our school lunches. Our sandwiches were wrapped in grease-proof paper, and we were required to bring the paper home each day and reuse it for the entire week's worth of sandwiches. By Friday there was nothing much left of the paper – it was limp and creased 'to billy-o', and our school chums snickered as they passed us on the way to the rubbish bin to deposit their wrappings. Oh, the shame of it all!

There were kids at school who frequently bought their lunches at the Tuck Shop – not us! We would watch forlornly as they left the classroom early to go pick up their fresh lunches. The only occasions we were allowed to buy *our* lunch at the Tuck Shop was on our birthdays. Unfortunately our younger sister's birthday fell in the Christmas holidays, so that meant only THREE times a year we left our classrooms early to grab our hot pie, packet of chips and a meringue – unless of course someone's birthday fell on a weekend.

I used to enjoy spending time with my grandparents – except when I had to go shopping with Grandma. She always looked out for the 'specials' and commented in a loud voice when she thought the prices she was looking at were 'ridiculous'. For years, even after we had moved to the country, Grandma would catch the bus each week to buy the 'specials' for us so that when we came to visit, we would go back home with a car boot loaded up with groceries!

But while we endured stapled-together-used-paper as notepads, Sunlight Soap instead of shampoo and 6d. per week pocket money, I observed something.

Dad soon acquired his own accountancy practice, we moved into an architect-designed house on a block of land with an amazing view. Money was regularly sent overseas to help missionaries in their work, and my grandmother was financially supported after Grandpa died. When I left home to attend Teachers College I didn't have to find a part-time job to pay my rent or living expenses, and one year Dad gave me a car so I could come home on weekends.

And something else I've noticed since those 'careful' days…I still turn off the lights when I leave the room, still make notes on used paper and almost always choose the 'specials' at the supermarket. I enjoy sharing what I have with others, and value family and relationships with others far beyond buying the latest plasma or computer.

What's more, so do my children!

Thanks Dad.

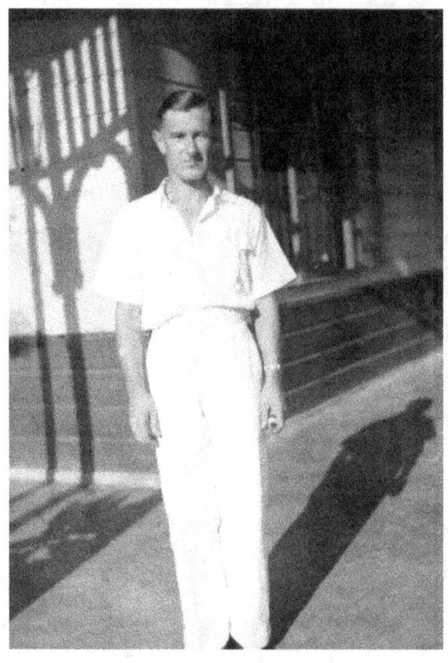 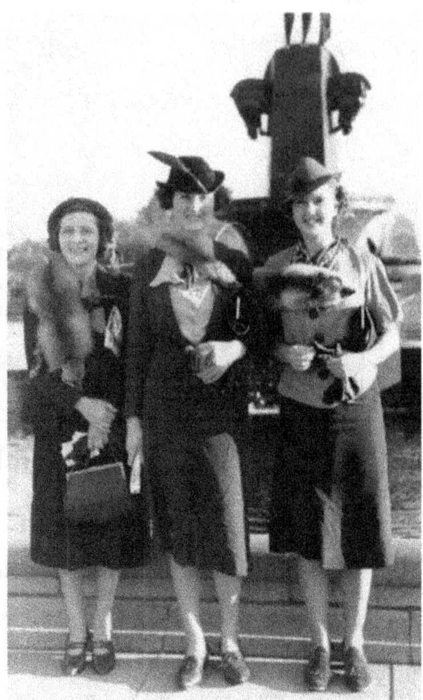

Alma first met Jack in the Paragon Milk Bar near Burwood Station in 1935. Her best friend, Edna, had asked Alma to accompany her while she met a bloke named Jim.

As it turned out Jim brought his mate, Jack, with him. Wow, he's nice looking, Alma thought when she first laid eyes on him. He had lightly tanned skin, the bluest of blue eyes and coal black hair. Of average height, he was slim and had an athletic body and he was 22. After milkshakes they walked down Burwood Road to the Picture Theatre.

The four of them got on well so they made arrangements to meet the following weekend at the local dance and so it went, until Edna and Jim broke up a few months later. Alma and Jack continued going out for two more years.

Theirs was a long distance romance with Jack working as a radio operator on a merchant navy ship, which meant he was away for six to eight weeks, then on shore for one or two weeks, then back out again.

'I am hoping to eventually get a shore job, working in aviation. I have a friend who works at AWA. He is going to let me know when something comes up. I will have to keep working on the ships until then,' Jack explained.

Alma liked the fact that Jack was ambitious and a bit of a go-getter. She also liked that he wasn't much of a drinker and loved dancing and swimming.

Whenever his ship came back to Sydney, he would catch the train out to Homebush, taking Alma to the local dance or the pictures. Sometimes they caught the train into Sydney, then the tram to Bondi Beach for a swim. Jack would sometimes borrow Alma's brothers push bike, and Alma, being a slim thing of twenty, would sit on a cushion on the handlebars while he peddled her around the suburb.

'I'm leaving next week for New Guinea to work on a copra ship. I'll be away for about three months this time,' Jack announced one visit.

She was becoming accustomed to this but it still put a damper on the romance. They would just start to get really close and he would be off again. She added it up once. In the two years they had known each other, they had actually only spent fifteen weeks together. I'm going to be an old maid forever, she thought, I'm 22 now and not even engaged.

Times had been tough on Jack. He'd come from New Zealand because of the Depression. He had no family here and he had to work. Making good money as a radio officer helped and he saved as much as he could, only spending his money on clothes and camera equipment. Free food and board was also a boon.

'I'm to catch the S.S. 'Montoro' to Port Moresby and pick up my ship there. Then it's straight to Rabaul where I'll be based. It will be three months before I see you again.' he said as he kissed her goodbye.

'Until next time, darling,' she said wistfully, as she waved him goodbye. They'd spent three weekends together and dinner at her home a few week nights in that time. She was really disappointed this time, three months was such a long time.

Alma worked as a secretary for an import agency. Luckily being part of a large family meant there were always people in the house. Her only brother who was the eldest had left home along with her two oldest sisters who had married. This left three daughters still living at home.

Edna and Phyllis, two unmarried girlfriends from Alma's school days, sometimes went out with her. She was also close to her younger sister Gwen, and they always had fun together.

Jack had been gone about six weeks and Alma began to wonder when his first letter would arrive. He always wrote as soon as he reached the first port, telling her little snippets of life on board the ships and of the ports he visited. He would write about how many whales he'd seen and anything that had happened on board. She always wrote back if she knew where he would be; telling him any news from home, knowing how much he looked forward to her letters.

How long would the mail take to get from Rabaul to Sydney by sea? It would most probably take about two or three weeks. Alma was anxiously expecting a letter any day now. She could hardly bear the waiting.

Finally, after two long months, a letter arrived from Jack. He'd posted it from Rabaul in Papua New Guinea. He'd been working on another ship for a month. He had been posted to another ship, the S.S. 'Durour' and was to board her in the morning. He promised to write when he arrived back in Rabaul. The ship would be collecting copra from small islands and he doubted if he could post anything.

Alma was so happy to receive this letter. She read it out to her family and proudly showed them the photo of Jack, taken outside the Pacific Hotel. The photo was given pride of place in a silver frame on her dressing table.

The months dragged on, with still no word from Jack. She began to wonder if the relationship was over but she knew Jack wasn't the type to break it off without telling her. It was well over four months since he sailed out and she had only one letter so far.

She discussed her fears with her sister Gwen while on the train to work one morning.

'Do you think he'll come back to me? Do you think he has found someone else in New Guinea?'

Ever the optimist, Gwen said, 'He'll come back to you. It's a well known fact that there aren't many women in New Guinea, Al. Anyway, none of them would be as good looking as you.'

A few more months dragged on. She thought his ship might have sunk or he'd met with an accident or something else sinister. The firm where she worked received all the shipping news and she meticulously scanned it; to no avail. There was no mention of his ship. Even though there were a few ships in that area, none had met with misadventure. She was left even more puzzled.

With a heavy heart she carried on as usual. What else could she do under the circumstances? She knew he had made it to Rabaul, but after that he seemed to have vanished into thin air.

One morning while on the train to work she opened the Sydney Morning Herald. The headlines screamed, 'Volcanic eruption in Rabaul – hundreds killed'. Oh my God! No! She couldn't believe it. The eruption had occurred at the end of May and it was now the middle of June. Her heart sank.

She read every word of the article carefully. Over four hundred people had been killed and the town was in ruins. A volcano had suddenly erupted in the middle of Blanche Bay in Rabaul Harbour. The whole town had been covered in pumice ash. The harbour was choked with the ash, which was well over six feet deep, making it hard for ships to get in and out. Those residents who survived the eruption were evacuated. The roads were impassable. The drinking water was contaminated. The houses had been crushed by the weight of the ash. A photo showed the harbour with a huge cloud of smoke filling the middle. There was also a picture of a car with ash piled high all over it.

She couldn't stop thinking about Jack all day. She felt sure his ship had been sailing around the islands picking up copra when the volcano erupted. He mentioned in his first letter they were taking copra back to Port Moresby to be shipped back to Australia. Why hadn't she received another letter? After all it was now nearly seven months since she had last seen him, with only one letter so far.

More months came and went. After looking at the newspaper article, her family doubted he would have survived the eruption if he had been in the harbour at the time. She nearly gave up hope of ever seeing Jack again. Her family stopped asking if she had heard anything as it only upset her more. She felt he must be alive somewhere, even though no one said anything. Her mother, who was psychic, suddenly declared one day, 'Jack is all right. He will just turn up one day as usual'.

Alma was still broken-hearted. In her heart he was 'the one'. But why hadn't he come back to Sydney? He'd always been so reliable. In the two years she'd known him, he'd always kept his word, writing and arriving, when he said.

She decided to go to the dance at the Strathfield Town Hall next Saturday with Gwen and Phyllis. Her mother, a dressmaker by trade, had cut out a new pale blue, shot-silk dress for her. Alma spent all weekend in front of the treadle sewing machine making sure it was finished on time.

The next Friday night, Alma and her family were in the lounge room listening to the radio as usual. They heard a sharp, loud knock on their front door. Alma's mother, Estelle said, 'I wonder who that could be Bill?' Then, looking around the big oak table, she asked, 'Was anyone expecting a visitor?' All three daughters shook their heads in unison.

'I'll get it,' said Gwen, racing up the hallway.

When she opened the door, there on the step, silhouetted against the street lamp, stood Jack. Gwen was so surprised she was speechless.

'Hello Gwen, can I come in?' asked Jack.

'Of course,' said Gwen, recovering quickly as she stepped aside, motioning him to go in.

He'd bought two bottles of cold beer to share with the family. This was a very welcome interlude to the night, which usually involved just sitting around listening to the radio, reading or playing the piano. Alma was so surprised and excited she threw her arms around his neck and gave him a resounding kiss on the lips.

'Hello, darling, did you miss me?' Jack asked cheekily, grinning from ear to ear. 'You'll never in a million years guess what has happened to me,' he added rather dramatically.

'It's been eight months since your last letter, Jack Faulkner. This had better be good.' Alma said, turning her back on him and sitting down at the dining room table, where she had been reading only five minutes ago. Her father Bill, sensing a good story, stood up and put out his hand.

'Welcome back. Take a seat Jack and tell us all about it. I'll get us all a glass and we'll have a drink while you tell us your story.'

'Thanks Bill, don't mind if I do.' Jack shook Bill's hand and sat down next to Alma. The rest of the family decided this was more exciting than anything else and gathered around the table.

'Well, I'll start at the beginning…

To be continued…(see 'Jack's back')

(Family photos – author)

Request to the heart surgeon - Gail Hennessy

Tomorrow you will be handling my lover's heart
go carefully and slowly

make sure that you have slept well
the night before and that your hands are steady

I believe you will stop his heart
I used to do that when we were young

or almost. I will be waiting outside
the theatre for your news ready to enter

the intensive care unit. You had best use
every skill at your finger tips. I ask

that you are methodical and astute
that you choose well the replacement

veins from his leg and stitch carefully
and when you enter his chest cavity

do so with utmost care. Slice, peel back
as you would soft fruit, meticulously, gently

be aware that you are mending two hearts
for his heart is also mine.

Chris was in charge of the moon - John McBride

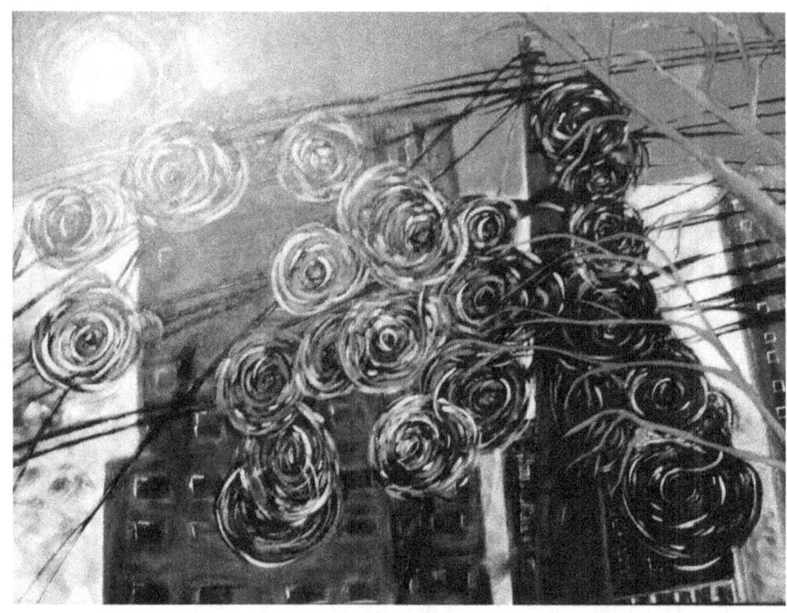

If you go outside and look in the sky, you will see the moon - up there - shining - spreading its magic - down on us. There is a small boy somewhere who looks after that moon. When my kids were little, the moon was looked after by my son Chris.

When your children are small, you enter a world of make-believe. No-one ever plans on this. It just happens. When Christmas time comes along, you find yourself telling the kids about the presents that Father Christmas is going to bring them. A few months later the Easter Bunny comes along and leaves them with Easter Eggs. When a tooth falls out, a dollar appears under the child's pillow that night, placed there by the Tooth Fairy. It was a wonderful world.

One Sunday afternoon we heard an enormous crash. We all rushed out in the front yard and saw a huge gumtree had fallen on the roof of our neighbours directly opposite. There were cars parked on the nature strip, the neighbour and his family looking white-faced and shocked, the SES men in their orange jackets. For the following weeks when I settled the kids down to bed at night with stories, I told the kids tales of the man who lived across the street from us. I told how at night he had to put a branch under his bed, so the Roof Fairy would come and fix his roof.

One year at Easter time, we camped in the Barmah State forest near the Murray River. It was a beautiful spot: flat open forest bed, tall wonderful gum trees all around. For safety reasons, we camped out in the open, away from the danger of falling branches. When we planned that camping trip we did not know they had a hunting season in that area. Through the night as we slept in our group of little dome tents, we heard gunshots in the distance. The gunfire was sporadic, but it kept up all night. Naturally we talked about it and reassured the kids. The next thing I knew we were discussing the Easter Bunny who was going to be visiting our tent overnight and leaving his eggs. It turned into a memorable night as we started to tell stories about how the Easter Bunny was going to get through, with his eggs, to our tent, with all those hunters firing.

Another time, my son Chris was small: four or five years old, and we were on a family camping trip at Mt Buffalo National Park in North East Victoria. It was dark and the moon was out -- shining all around, so that we could walk in the bush and see everything in the moonlight. I suspect we must have been up there camping that year at Easter time, possibly to get away from the hunters and to increase the Easter Bunny's chances of getting through to us with his eggs.

After setting up camp, I decided to go for a walk.

'I'm going for a walk. Does anyone want to come?'

'I'll come Dad.'

'Did you have fun today, setting up camp?'

'Yes. I helped put up my tent.'

'Yes, I saw. You were a big help. Did your big sister Lyn put the pegs in the ground, or did you do it yourself?'

'I did one peg, and Lyn did the others.'

'Do you like it up here at Mt Buffalo?'

'Yes.'

'Look at those white trees. See how their trunks shine white. Those trees are called snow gums. When you see trees with white trunks and branches like that, remember they are snow gums.'

'Look at the moon…Isn't it bright? Do you think it's the same moon we have back in Beaumaris?'

'Yes.'

'So how did it get here from Beaumaris? Did you bring the moon?'

'Yes….I put it up there.'

'I told you to bring your toys and something to sleep with. I didn't realise you were going to bring the moon.'

Next year at Christmas time: *'OK everybody start packing your bag of books and toys for the camping trip. We leave early in the morning. Lyn, make sure you pack the beach ball and your tennis set. Chris, bring your new farmyard set. Chris, don't forget the moon!'*

One year on a family holiday in the United States…standing on the rim of the Grand Canyon:

'Kids, isn't this great……Chris, did you bring the moon?' -- Chris takes his hands out of his pockets and points up.

Another year, I worked in Berlin, Germany, for six months visiting the Free University. There are many amazing memories. Late one afternoon on a weekend, walking through the Grunewald forest in the Berlin suburbs, surrounded by forest, feeling the scent of the pine tree twigs underfoot as we walked – and there ahead of us, near the horizon, the moon bright and round:

'Chris, is that your moon?'

And once there was a time when the moon had to weave its magic. It was during our six months in Europe, late in the European autumn of 1989. It was a time of general unrest with demonstrations and civil protests going on across the group of countries known then as Eastern Europe. We know now that eventually the protestors and demonstrators had their way. Later that year governments fell, with the most well publicised event being the fall of the Berlin wall. But while it was happening, no-one knew how it was going to end. My wife, three kids and I were visiting Prague, a magical place of medieval streetscapes. Central to the city is an ancient bridge spanning the river, known as the Charles Bridge. The Charles Bridge is one of the highlights of Europe, with guard towers and great Baroque style statues along each side.

While we were walking the Bridge and admiring it, we could hear a background sound of a loud crowd. In the distance, on the next bridge along, we could see the silhouette of a crowd surging and calling. On the opposite side of the bridge we could see the gleam of helmets and shields of a military style police force. While we walked and looked at the statues and the elaborate structures on the bridge, the two opposing forces on the next bridge down surged towards one another and crashed. The kids did not seem to notice this, so we continued along with them, through the narrow streets of the old town, working our way back towards the rail station to travel to our apartment in the suburbs.

As we walked, the background sound of the rioting and fighting picked up in volume, so I was beginning to worry about our safety. Through it all, we chatted to the kids, asking about the fairy-book castle they had visited that day. I spotted a restaurant as we walked. We all went inside, and sat in a beautiful historic setting, at an old wooden table in front of a wrought iron window frame. We ate pancakes with fruit and syrup while the demonstrators rushed past outside the window, with police in riot helmets chasing after them. As we sat and watched, we could see Chris's moon through the window. So we talked about the moon, and we discussed how marvellous it was that Chris was doing such a good job bringing the moon with him, even here to Prague.

There were many trips and many stories. We camped every year at Mt Buffalo. We travelled to Bali Indonesia several times, where we stayed in a losmen in a small village and walked the rice fields. Always Chris brought the moon, and put it up in the sky to watch down on us as we walked.

Chris was born in March at the end of the 1982-83 El Nino; so he must be 27 years old now. He has grown up and is too old to be in charge of the moon. I expect the responsibility has been passed on to someone else. I don't know how these things work, whether it has to be an Australian child, or even a Melbourne child. But I would like to think that somewhere there is a small child. When his or her parents tell the child to pack a bag to take on the family camping holiday, the child has the responsibility of bringing the moon.

The yellow wading pool - Jennifer Goard

The 'Olympic Village' Melbourne, a place of run down, two storied, red bricked flats, home to the poor and down trodden was my home in 1967.

I lived with my mum, my sister, who was eighteen months older than me, my baby brother and sometimes my dad. Dad was in the Navy so we were living in the Commission home.

We had a yellow, canvas wading pool, which had metal legs and poles which slid through the sides to hold it up, and had the added benefit of stopping the water falling out. It must have been a cow of a thing to put up, because Mum would swear a lot and turn a crazy shade of crimson while attempting the job.

One very hot Melbourne day, we pleaded and nagged her to put the pool up. Our begging fell on deaf ears. However, my siblings and I were persistent. Finally she relented. After a lot of grunting, cursing, and sweating in the overheated backyard, Mum gave in and filled the pool. We ran with great anticipation to put our bathers on. We jumped into the pool.

'*Don't you kids dare come inside!* You make sure to stay out there in that pool,' were her departing words as she slammed the back door.

Melbourne is always guaranteed a cool change, or any change really. Thick, black storm clouds gathered over our little back-yard, threatening doom. Lightening flew across the roof of the flat. Thunder rumbled. The wind roared under our canvas pool, making the water vibrate.

Screaming in terror, with thunder on our tails, the three of us fell over ourselves getting out of the pool. We raced, shivering and frightened to the wooden screen door, only to find that Mum had locked it.

We wailed in unison, 'Let us in,' we wailed in unison, crying desperately at the sheer injustice.

'You can stay out in that bloody pool! You begged all day to have it up. Now stay out there!' was Mum's angry response.

The next set of thunder cracked even louder over our heads than before. We screamed like blue murder. Mum finally came and let us inside.

We must have outdone the thunder itself.

A tribute to grandparents - Julie Cochrane

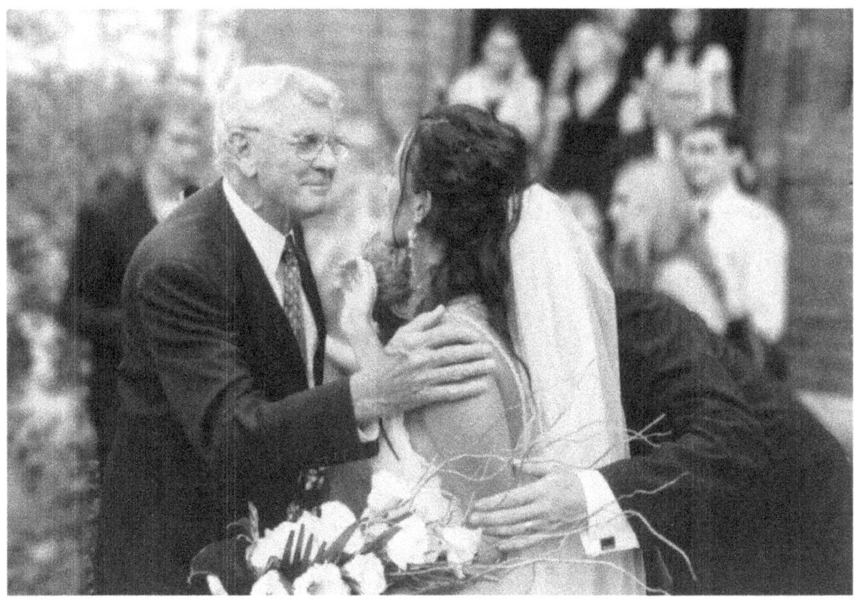

'*Awakening occurs in different ways: when we have new understanding about who we are in the universe, or when we see that our life is vastly bigger than we ever thought.*' *(Duane Elgin)*

I experienced an Awakening the day my first grandchild was born—grandparenthood. I had often wondered how this moment would feel. I had asked other Grandmothers, but they rarely found the right words to explain.

'*You'll just have to wait and see for yourself*', they would say.

Having had wonderful grandparents myself, and, as a child having been greatly loved and influenced by my paternal grandparents in particular, I was looking forward to the experience.

I have also witnessed the joy and richness that has been added to my own children's lives through their relationship with their grandparents and this added to the happy expectation of becoming a Grandparent.

I wasn't disappointed.

Having now become Grandmother to three amazing grandsons and 1 absolutely beautiful granddaughter, I, like my friends, find it difficult to give expression to our relationship.

Suffice it to say, that I absolutely *love* being 'Nanny'. To my grandchildren I am their No.1 supporter and cheerleader for the rest of my natural life.

I *cannot* for the life of me understand why their parents are so mean and unreasonable when it comes to silly things like not eating their vegetables, or drawing pictures all over their body with Texta pen.

Yes, an Awakening has occurred in my life and I am embracing it wholeheartedly, enjoying my 'vastly bigger' life with great delight.

A couple of years ago my daughter wrote about the special place my parents, her grandparents, play in her life.

With her permission, I share it with you…

Memories of Nan and Pa by Rachel Bennett

If only the walls of my grandparent's house could speak. There is a certain nostalgic smell that can only be smelled there. And every time I walk in the front door I can detect it. The house is filled with memories – smells and sights and sounds. I can hear laughter and my Pa's footsteps thumping up the stairwell chasing us kids.

I can hear the word, 'mugwamp' – his favourite name for us – as he catches us and picks us down, tickling us rotten and licking our ears! I can see Nan busily making treats in the kitchen. 'Are you hungry darling?' she asks, and whereas in reality the answer is 'no', we find ourselves answering, 'Yes' – always curious what exactly she was offering.

I hear laughter, stories told. There are secret places that all we grandkids know about, down under the stairs. Armed with a spotlight, our adventures would begin and our imaginations would run wild. My brother and I went down there again recently and laughed as we found some old, yellowed drawings we had left there years ago.

Often my brother and I would sneak into bed with Nan as she was being served breakfast by her handsome waiter, Pa. Vegemite toast and a cup of tea was always on the menu. We would spend what seemed like all morning talking and laughing and giggling over silly things. I would love Nan's nightgowns and always thought she looked so beautiful and elegant.

I spent the night before my wedding in that bed. Nan and Pa had offered their house for me and my bridesmaids to prepare for my wedding while they stayed elsewhere. It had always been my dream as a little girl to leave from their house on my wedding day. I remember lying there in that bed praying for my marriage to be like theirs. I wanted to love the way they loved. I wanted to respect and honour my husband Joel, the way Nan had Pa. I wanted to raise awesome children who knew and loved God the way they had raised their children. I am truly blessed to have witnessed such a strong marriage.

There really is no one like my Nan and Pa. I have watched their life together, their love for each other and their walk with God. I am blessed because of them. They have a legacy to pass on which I believe God is proud of. They are a man and woman of faith, honesty, kindness, generosity, compassion, wisdom and gratitude. I pray my life honours that which they have instilled in me. There really is no place like home. Although we all have our own houses, the one place we love to congregate most is in Nan and Pa's home.

I trust one day my grandchildren will be able to write about their relationship with me, *their* grandmother, with the same passion, love and respect.

(Photograph for this story – Julie Cochrane)

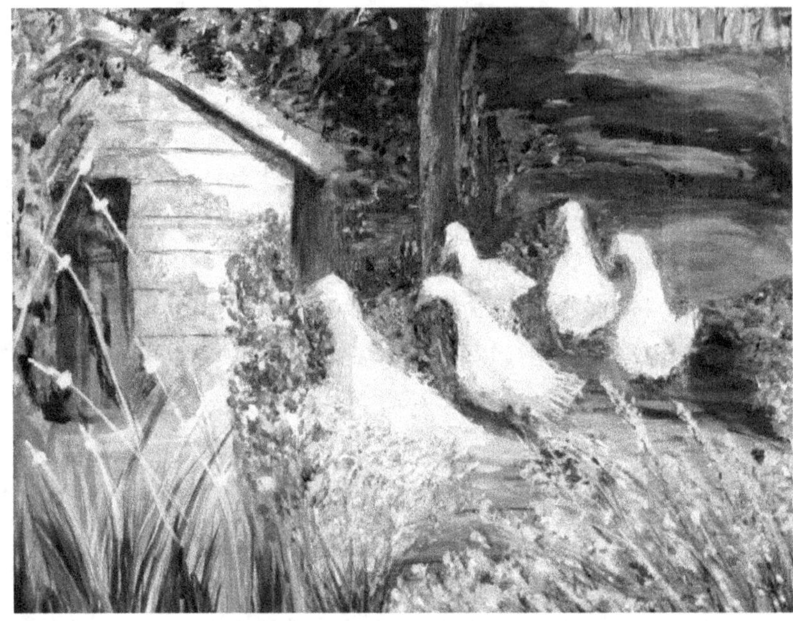

Much is made of the carefree life of the Fifties and Sixties. The time of security of a neighbourhood where everyone knew each other. A time of innocence and social safety, freedom to roam. But there was a downside.

From the echelons of the rich to the parsimony of the poor there was a dearth. A lack of explanation, a void in teaching children about life. It seemed that generation after generation had learned by experience and that was how the world worked. It didn't work for our generation and many times I have wondered if it had ever really worked. The idea that Life would bring the lessons you needed, neatly wrapped, delivered to your doorstep at just the time you needed them, that no-one needed to answer questions, explain life, emotions or relationships.

For me, and I suspect for many others, it was an unbearable silence that confused and complicated life. What you're not told, you guess. Some brush things aside, some experiment and others pursue the knowledge of oneself with exuberance via drugs, sex and Rock'n'Roll.

'Finding yourself' was the catchcry of the Seventies. Parents were mystified. How could we be lost inside ourselves? What the hell were we looking for?

I buried myself in serving others and in enough self analysis to 'find' myself as well as a few thousand other people. But all I found was confusion. In my naivety I shared that confusion with friends and family who found my observations far less attractive than their own thoughts. In their opinion no-one needed to think quite that much about *anything*, not even nuclear physics, much less how to 'be' in the world.

The little that was said to us about emotions gave the distinct impression that they were unnecessary, untrustworthy and generally to be avoided. Emotions were flaws. If they reared their ugly heads they were to be subjugated with all possible force. Bringing them up in public was akin to bringing up wind, and about as attractive. If you *must* have them—keep them to yourself; after all, that's what the Queen does, along with all civilised people.

I seemed to be particularly unfortunate, in that I was afflicted with more emotions than any self-respecting person would lay claim to. I made matters worse by seeking answers with all the zeal and persistence of Oliver Twist's quest for more porridge. I learned that there was only one thing worse than the pursuit of 'answers' and that was to ask 'what's wrong with wanting to know stuff?'

Babies cried a lot. Children cried occasionally. Adults never cried. It was apparently something that you grew out of, like the desire to suck your thumb. I found my father crying behind our dunny when I was a little girl and Dad's pet rabbit had died. He was ashamed of his tears and turned away from me. The world spun on its axis. Everything I thought I knew about emotions was ripped away.

Mum's sister died and she howled like a cow in labour and I wasn't allowed near her until the outpouring of her grief was over. I wanted to make her better so I stood by her door and sang her favourite song that always made her happy—'I'll fly away'. I was sent away from her doorway. The world went from turning on its axis to spinning out of control.

I called my cat to come home and it was hit by a car. I ran to where my father had gone to cry. My brother's dog licked me and I held him with vice-like fingers, howling in agony and wondering when the magic of 'growing up' happened and emotions left you alone. Ever after I cried alone and vowed no-one would ever see my tears, my secret shame.

I grew older and nursed the dying and still I cried alone, confused.

I married and gave birth to a premature baby who died. Then I cried everywhere with everyone. There was no longer a place to hide. There was also no place to put the pain, the grief, the emotions. No map to guide, no creed to explain, no answer worthy of the question.

After two months, the air was still dark and too dense to breathe. I was exhorted to 'get over it', 'snap out of it' or 'pull myself together'. Useless, useless words.

There was no other explanation than the glaring fact that I must be flawed. I wasn't normal. I phoned my GP and gave her this very clever self-diagnosis and she talked to me. She had also buried a son. She asked a few simple questions about how I felt; then gave me the profound gift of the truth.

'You're doing everything you should be doing. This is how life is. It's okay. This is the way it will be for a bit longer. You're supposed to cry, to grieve. You have experienced the unthinkable. You have suffered loss. Don't let anyone tell you not to cry.' I was reprieved. I had permission to cry. But so much more—permission to feel, permission to be human, alive and unrestrained.

Sometime later I heard a laugh. It had a familiar sound, yet, was somehow strange. It was an echo of something past, a promise of things to come. Where had it come from? I touched my hand to my throat. It had come from me. Life had bubbled to the surface again. Joy had revisited me.

I gave myself permission to laugh, permission to live. There was no other part of me to find. I had found all of myself.

Give me permission to cry, and you empower me to laugh; to live.

(Geese in backyard – Louise Sauer)

People and Community

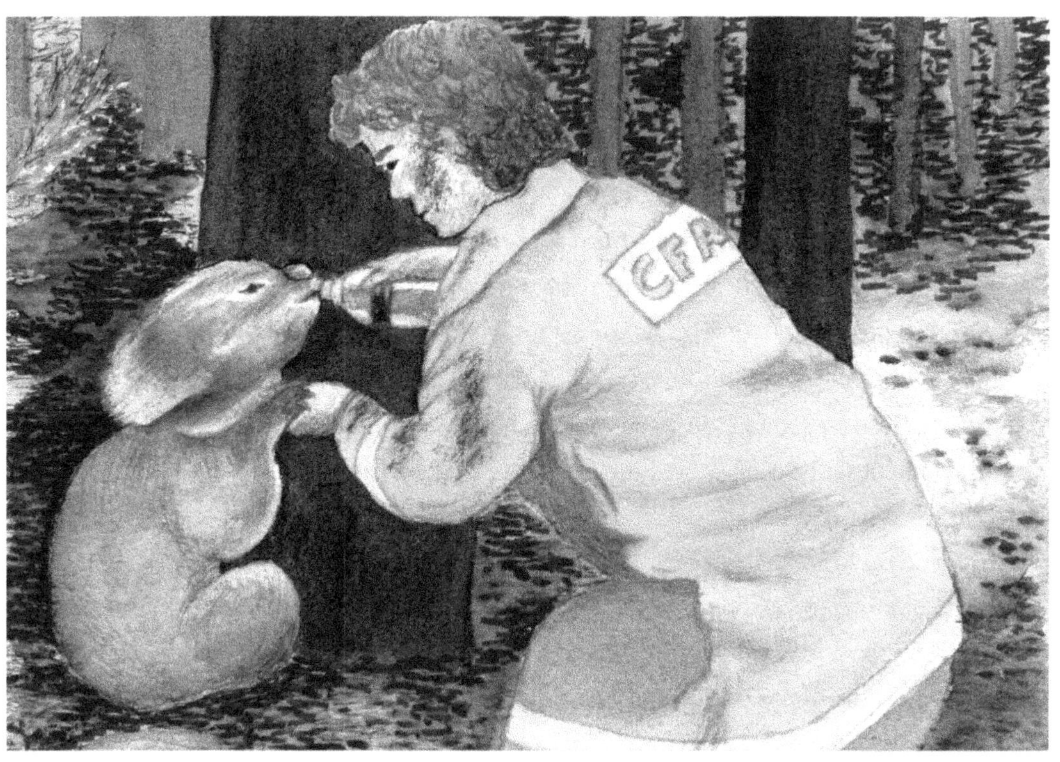

Census – Bush Style - Linda Visman

Liz, Helen and I were teachers in a remote indigenous community 330 kilometres from Alice Springs. The road was mostly sand – hard packed and corrugated when dry, soft and boggy when wet. In August 1991, we became collectors for the National Census. We'd never done one in an urban community, let alone out bush, and knew we'd be earning our meagre pay. However, we thought it would be a great way of getting to know the families in the communities better.

Most people didn't know their dates of birth, so we had to use data given to us by the clinic at Urapuntja, near Utopia, the nearest medical clinic, eighty kilometres away. The records, we noticed, showed an awful lot of people born on the first of January. However, we quickly realised that this was a generic date for those who had no record of birth. They'd all been born before white man's officialdom reached that part of the world so the actual year they were born was an estimate.

Up to 1961, all births were recorded as the first of January. In 1961 there were a couple on the first of June. These were probably babies born some time during that year. It looked like records only began on paper in 1962 or 1963. From 1963, they showed the actual date of birth. These records were important for us at school too, as they were the only source of information on how old our pupils were. Most parents didn't know - after all, dates had no significance to them. It was the seasons, the bush tucker and the ceremonies that were important in their lives.

The government statistician wanted the census for people living in our remote communities, as well as in the towns and cities. Helen elected to be the co-ordinator. A few weeks before the census date, she had to get the list of family groups who lived in the area. I think there were about four or five, as practically everyone was related. There was a lot of paperwork to be done: an overall community list; a form for each household; and a form for each person in the household.

We worked on the forms over several days before and after the census. Helen went out to Irrultja, forty-five kilometres away, to do their forms, Liz did the tiny communities at Antarringinya and Ngkwarlalanima, ninety and eighty kilometres away. We had remote classrooms at these outstations, and I did Ampilatwatja, the hub community and the largest in the area.

'Hi Bob. Hi Jen. Can we go through the census form together?'

'Okay. What we gotta do?'

'Let's sit down and I'll show you.'

We all sit in the red dirt in front of the tin house. A couple of dogs approach to check me out, and

Bob casually kicks them aside. Bob and Jen work at the school. They understand English well and can read a little, better than most in the community, but not enough to decipher the ins and outs of the census form.

'How old are you, Bob?'

'Don't know. Might be forty. Maybe forty-five. Something like that.'

'What about you, Jen?'

'About forty I think. Might be 1950-something.'

'What if I look up the clinic records and find out? Is it okay if I fill that in later?'

'Yeah. That's all right.'

'Shall I do that for the kids too – all four of them?'

'Yeah. You can check them out and write it for us.'

We went through the questions.

Language used at home (Alyawarra). Employment. Income range. Where they lived last census. Religion?

'We traditional people. Got no religion. But sometimes we go to that Baptist preacher when he comes around. Sometimes talk with Lutheran too.'

'I'll put down traditional, shall I?'

'Yeah. That's right for us.'

'And I'll put down that you identify as Aboriginal. Okay?'

'Sure, that's okay.' He laughs and holds out his dark brown arm. 'Look at this skin, must be Aboriginal, eh?'

We went through communities, sitting at each house, shack or camp with the head of the family, wives, children and dogs hanging about, eager to see their details written on this important document. We were surprised at the age of some of the people at Ampilatwatja. Out of the men, only three, all brothers, were over fifty-five. One died a few months later. I suppose we shouldn't have been surprised, because with two or more wives each, they were the fathers and grandfathers of most of the community. Several women were over seventy. I don't know what their real names were. Even though they had their traditional names, English names were given to them by station owners or were adopted by the people themselves for simplicity, and these are the names by which all official agencies know them.

About one hundred and fifty people came and went during the several days it took to go to each camp and house within the community to get the information needed to complete the census forms. Sometimes I had to go back a couple of times to see the head of the household who might have been away hunting when I called before. Or they might have all been off at another community visiting relatives. Then, when we had done all we could, the paperwork was completed and assembled, and Helen sent it all off to the Census people in Alice Springs.

It was an interesting exercise for us. Even though Liz and I had been in the community for almost two years, we didn't know everyone properly. We knew the school children and their immediate families, the elders and their wives but, with movement between outstations, others were not always around. The census gave us the opportunity to talk with people in their own environment, not in the alien ones of the school or Council meetings. We learned more about them on a personal level, and they learned more about us as well. We had been 'adopted' into the community a few months after we arrived in January 1990 and were given skin names that made us related in a particular way – mother, grandmother, sister, aunt, daughter – to everyone in the community, and we learned more about our actual relationships with every individual. After all, they were our second family.

(Names have been changed for privacy and cultural reasons)

The Great Homework Swindle: - Matthew Glenn Ward

Time takes an eternity when you're 12. Especially when you take a day off school. Not doing homework in the late 1970s meant sore hands and wounded pride, and those suffering such indignities never seemed to learn. I was one of those occasional homework defaulters and my plan of 'wopping' school as we called it seemed a good one at 8am on the morning the Mathematics homework was due.

Anyway, some back story. In 1979 I was in my first year of high school at the old St Pius X College Adamstown (Newcastle NSW Australia). The older, white building with the zig-zag roof used to be an underwear factory in the 1950s where my mum used to work as a clerk. I believe in the 1960s it was sold to the Catholic Church and there they established St Pius X College, an all boys secondary school that only admitted girls in the mid-1980s. Chattering sewing machines were replaced with priests, desks, blackboards, crucifixes and chattering students.

I had an uncle who attended 'Pius' in the '60s, but most of the males in my family went to Marist Brothers Hamilton, in 'Town' as we called inner city Newcastle (and still do). But we lived in New Lambton, a lot closer to Pius than 'Marist' so when given the choice of schools I chose Pius, mainly because of distance.

Maths was never my signature event. English, History, even Science came easy to me but the mystery of numbers always baffled me because I had to *try* and I was lazy. And because I was lazy I would conveniently 'forget' to do homework related to certain subjects I couldn't stand. Maths was one of those subjects.

So one cold Newcastle morning I packed up my black sports bag with books and headed not to the bottom field entrance of the college but instead to the corner store on the Bridges Road side of Alder Park to wait until that Maths class was over. My theory was that the homework would be dealt with by our teacher Mr Ron 'Lefty' Wright and I would not have to do it.

The little shop was called 'Louie's' by everyone we knew. It was run by a kind man of European extraction called Louie. The name 'Nantsou' was painted on the wall out front so I gathered his name was Louie Nantsou. Made sense to me even at that young age. My nan, when she lived in New Lambton about a quarter of a kay away, used to send me on errands to buy the essentials: bread, butter, milk, sometimes Devon, and also Benson & Hedges cigarettes. She used to call Louie up to tell him I was on my way. I'd hand over a $10 paper bill and Louie would hand me the groceries.

Back in 1979 one could get a small bottle of Coke or Fanta for 17 cents, believe it or not. So on this crisp morning at 8am I walked into Louie's shop, bought a small bottle of Fanta and sat down on a cold, metal fold-up promotional Coke chair. I slowly sipped the Fanta, and glanced every now and then at my 9th birthday Lauris watch. Class started at 9am. History was first (with teacher, Mr Smyth, a former Spitfire pilot). Then Geography (Mr Mulconry). Finally Maths. So that was 2 and a half hours for me to wait!

I chatted with Louie about business (as if I knew what I was talking about). I might have bought a second bottle of drink, (I cannot remember). I would have looked at the array of canned goods on the shelves, the customers who walked in and out, and the traffic that bounded up Bridges Road towards the old Garden City shopping centre in Kotara. Finally, I left, thanking Louie on my way out.

I dawdled back along the road, past Alder Park Bowling Club, the old Caltex service station, under the overhead train bridge, through the gate and across the bottom football field. I ambled across the stormwater canal bridge, looked up and was surprised to see boys out playing when they still should have been in class.

I saw one of my friends and he asked me where I was. I made something up, like I was sick. I asked him why everyone was out of class and he said that because of the sports carnival later in the week, the timetable was changed to Tuesday's, and they were having an early lunch. (The Maths class I was hoping to miss didn't even happen.)

When I did go to the next Maths class, a few days later (my mind is hazy on this but I believe) I cobbled together something in the way of homework to show the teacher, but he had forgotten and we moved on to something else.

The heart remembers - Linda Brooks

An apology for the Forgotten Children.

There is no sorrow deeper than the sorrow of unknowing
the sorrow of a truth denied.
While broad willows weep, we too lend our tears,
for those who travelled alone,
their childhood innocence stolen,
waiting for the heartache of generations
to be acknowledged, shared.
There are many to blame;
systems, departments, churches,
but ultimately people
their eyes closed, ears covered
to the voiceless,
abandoned, abused and forgotten.
It could have been us,
but it was you.
And it is you we will thank,
survivors all;
for finding courage,
for bringing outrage.
For hanging on, when the nation let go.
For speaking, when the world was silent.
Today we applaud you, celebrate and
remember you.

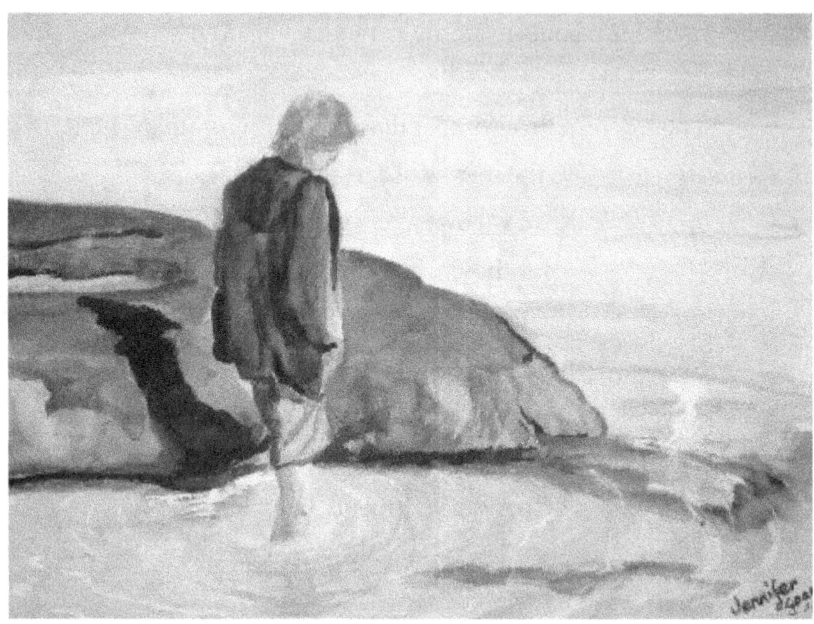

'Jesus' walked along the shoreline; the pure white Chelsea sands that squished beneath his bare feet massaged him as he went.

The sky was the bluest of blue, the sun in the heavens above, sent shafts of light to warm his body as he moved cat-like along the sand. The crystal clear water lapped against his ankles sending shivers of happiness up his spine. He rejoiced in the sensual pleasure of the beauty which surrounded him. He did a little dance to celebrate his happiness.

Jesus' blue denim jeans had been chopped off at the knees where the fabric had become thin and faded with time, the frayed edges encircled his tanned legs like frilly halos. He had a preference to sling his white t-shirt casually over his left shoulder, hanging there by itself as if with divine adhesive.

He wore a leather thong around his neck and a spiralling shell sat comfortably between his collar bones just below his Adam's apple, which would move up and down when he spoke.

His hair was a shocking knotted mane and had been bleached white by the ever present sun. Wayward strands standing out haphazardly from his scalp illuminated the delicate features of his face, which was covered around his chin by a gentle fuzz.

His eyes were the same colour as the summer sky and held the depths of the universe in them.

His body was a collection of sculptured muscles; thin and wiry, giving him the profile of a middle weight fighter, lean but strong.

In his right hand, he kept a black, bound Bible with many book marks poking out of the pages, reminders of what had transpired for him the last time he was on earth.

During the summer of '79, Jesus became a common sight on our beach. He would strut past the Life Saving Club on his mission from God, and make his way gradually towards the jetty stopping frequently to preach at the sunbaking sinners lying on their colourful towels.

Once he had been given eye contact by the sinners on the colourful towels, he would squat down on his haunches and begin to warn the sinners on the beach about his arch nemesis 'The Great Horned One' and how if they did not listen to him – being the son of god and all – 'The Devil' would find them and torment them in eternal hell. He would open his battered bible to a pre-selected page and read a verse or two to back up his opinions.

After the reading he told them that he needed them to accept him and his dad into their lives and believed that a donation would help in this matter.

Most of the time Jesus was ordered to 'piss off or they would call the police' by the people he preached to. He would then bless them with the sign of his cross, stand up and proceed to move away from the angry ones to start again further along the beach.

I guess people just didn't want to know or listen to his word.

One beautiful morning, on a classically beautiful Chelsea beach day, my friends from the Life Saving Club and I had parked ourselves on our towels in front of 'The Club' and giggled as we watched Jesus make his way towards us.

With his bible in his right hand and T-shirt hanging from his shoulder, he squatted down on the sand beside us and immediately started to speak to us about his father in heaven, who he missed very much, and about the hatred he felt from people of his being here.

'How come you are here?' someone near me asked him.

'I have returned to give everyone a second chance. I have come back to save you all.' He told us in his rich flowing voice sounding the entire world like angels singing.

'Oh right,' we all said together and nodded our heads in acknowledgement of his statement, looking at each other with a knowing – he's kind of crazy- way.

'How do you know you are Jesus?' asked my younger brother, who happened to be sitting with us, his question laced with poisonous cynicism.

'Well,' Jesus replied, 'I was eating some bread and chipped my tooth on a stone that had been baked into it, just as it says in the bible.' Then he opened his bible to the exact page and read us an excerpt proving the point he had just made. He had fire in his eyes as he read and you could see he was consumed with passion for who he was.

Towards the end of the summer season, Jesus was taken away from the beach by the police. They came down onto the blazing hot sand in their uniforms, one on each arm leading him away. Someone had complained about Jesus and his teachings. As the little group passed us, we looked up at them from our colourful towels in our place in front of 'The Club', and Jesus blessed us.

Jesus seemed harmless enough to me, a gentle fool or a crazy bloke who had stumbled upon our paradise, finding sceptics and sinners on the beach at Chelsea. The concept of Jesus is safe whilst being invisible or as a plaster figure planted firmly on a cross on the walls of our churches, but to have him walk around in the flesh—well this constitutes madness in our society and is not tolerated by the powers that be.

Jesus didn't return to our beach at the beginning of the new century.

('Jesus' – Jennifer Goard)

The plane's stewardess was showing the passengers how to put on the life jackets and oxygen masks when it happened. I was sitting in one of the four seats in the middle aisle about half way down, and we were taxiing down the runway.

The plane had been delayed by half an hour already, because a lady sitting next to the window one row in front of my seat had called for a service man to come and fix the side wall of the plane. Apparently, according to her, she was in danger of being sucked out of her seat because part of the wall was not attached where it should have been.

Mary, from Amsterdam, who was sitting next to me, just rolled her eyes in my direction, to indicate this was unbelievable. She was a lovely-looking, blonde girl with beautiful tanned skin and was wearing extremely short denim shorts with frayed edges and a tight white T-shirt. Let's face it, she was gorgeous.

Anyway, they managed to finally get a man in overalls to come in with his tool box and put the offending part back into place. I was a tad worried about being sucked out of the plane myself, as I was on the aisle just one row back, so I would have gone out just after her companion. The woman who had complained was a very large woman, who would be squished if she had to get sucked out of that tiny little spot, about a foot square. I thought if *she* gets sucked out *that* little hole, then the rest of us are in big trouble and would be all sucked out in fairly quick succession. Not a nice thought at all.

What next? I thought. The stewardess had everyone put their seat belts on and prepare for take-off. The plane started taxiing down the runway, turned and was revving up its engines in readiness for take-off. About time.

Suddenly, the people three rows in front of me were standing up and yelling out. I couldn't hear what they were saying because of the roar of the engines. The stewardesses came running down the aisle telling everyone to stay in their seats. What now!!!

Then I heard a women, who was standing up and waving her arms frantically around, yell out, 'My dad's fainted! He's been vomiting!'

Oh great, I thought. Then I smelled the acrid smell of vomit. She's right, he had vomited. The plane came to a standstill in the middle of the runway. Mary asked the passenger next to her to move so she could get out because she was a nurse, and she would have a look at the sick man. Next thing, a doctor, who said he was an Emergency Specialist, came running down from the first class compartment to help out. He looked like an Italian Prince, he was so handsome. He had shoulder length dark brown hair and lovely tanned skin and big dark eyes. Whipping a stethoscope out of the medical bag he had brought with him, he bent down over the sick man. The doctor and Mary spoke softly while they hovered over him for a few minutes, and then the doctor said, 'This man is having a stroke. He has to go to hospital immediately'.

Great, I thought, this is going to take hours. The plane, having stopped virtually mid take-off, had to turn back to the terminal we had left half an hour before. Then we all waited. The Customs people had to come on and check the man and his son's identity. His son was going to accompany him to the hospital. They had to get their baggage out of the hold—no mean feat finding it amongst a plane load. An ambulance had been called. The man was helped to the plane door, put on a stretcher and taken to hospital. After another hour and a half we were off again.

By the time we actually left the runway, the plane was over two hours late. The Stewardess gave the doctor a free bottle of champagne for his part. She also told Mary there was a spare seat in First Class if she would like to sit up there for the duration of the flight. She thought that would be nice, grabbed her things and left.

The doctor and Mary were again called on mid-flight to put someone on a drip. The doctor hung the saline solution from the button handle on the overhead locker. He was not only handsome but resourceful as well. Someone mentioned the patient was a diabetic. He and Mary made a beautiful couple.

I'd had enough of planes and mid flight, I really just wanted to go home and NOW. Of course it was impossible.

The next flight I took was to Hawaii. However, when the whole plane was fully loaded with passengers, the Captain made an announcement. The plane would take off at least half an hour late due to a grey bird being sucked into the engine as it taxied to the terminal prior to take-off. Not again!!! The engineers were extracting the bird from the engine at that very moment. then they would turn the engine on to test it out for five minutes, then giving it a rest for five minutes, then testing it for a further five minutes, and rest it again before actually taking off.

All the passengers agreed it would be a good thing to GET THAT BIRD OUT. Eventually, they extracted what was left of the bird, tested the engine and we took off half an hour late. The rest of that flight was uneventful.

On the way back home however, we got to Honolulu Airport and were told to go to the end of the line to check in our baggage. The line was so long we couldn't see the end of it. Up to the back of the line we trudged, with our very overweight bags. We were told the computers were down and everyone had to be checked in by hand. They had to write out all the baggage labels and booking tickets by hand. Great.

We were speculating about how much we would be charged for excess baggage, expecting a massive bill after our spend-up in Las Vegas. We bought our whole family Reeboks at the factory outlet there. Finally we reached the counter ready to face the scales. The nice girl behind the counter told us they weren't charging for excess baggage due to the computers being down. Bonus.

We had thought we'd be charged for sure, and had taken some things out of our suitcases and put them into our hand luggage to even out the weight. They told us we could put as much of our luggage into the hold as we liked. We put our hand luggage in as well, so we wouldn't have to carry it until after the flight. Another bonus.

Our euphoria lasted only a short while. We waited and waited in the holding lounge for over two hours before the plane could be boarded. Instead of leaving at 8.15am, we didn't leave until 11.30am. The flight was also uneventful, no doubt due to my prayers to God to keep us safe, free of harm and happy.

I was telling one of the girls at work about all these delays and she looked at me for a moment before replying, 'So – *it's you then!*'

Really! As if I was a jinx or something!

To an Autistic Child - Gail Hennessy

Little butterfly
enclosed in the cocoon
of your own shadowed world.

How can I reach you, little shadow?

Locked in a silent nightmare
you scream my name.
Your one word—my name
not ever with joy
but always in searching.

Scarred knees from too many falls
stumbling steps behind your quicksilver brothers.

Dance little shadow
smile to the colours of the music
grasp the bright notes.

Please little shadow
turn around to face the light.

Too soon the pale light of the sun left the sky, its tired form dropping beyond the line of the western horizon.

Evening flowed in from the east dragging her cloak of stars behind her, covering the land and all that lay upon it. The sky changed from indigo to black as she went. A gentle fog, rolled in from off the bay, following the darkness and encompassing the low lying swamplands which surround my home, covering them with pale white mists.

On a cold winter's evening, such as this, the Bonbeach football oval seems to gather these swirling mists towards it, calling, beckoning wispy clouds to conceal it from the rest of the world. Hidden away by the fog, silence descends on the oval. Time ceases to exist in the tiny playing paddock.

Above the blanket of grey steel towers soar into the evening sky. Suddenly, as the heavy-duty globes are switched on the darkness turns into brilliant light, shining like mini suns across the frosty ground.

Silver gulls, on their journey back to the sea from the local rubbish tips become disorientated by the sudden brightness. They gather around the towers, fluttering like gigantic moths, their soulful screeching brandishing the night.

Not long after the lights go on with their garish beams bouncing off the seemingly impenetrable barrier of fog the ghostly voices begin. Slowly at first they filter up from the ground, through the barrier, into the atmosphere and across the fences of the neighbouring houses. Where we, in our homes can hear them.

Footy training has commenced.

Subdued commands from unseen men grow louder and rise from under the doona of fog.

'Kick it to me! Kick it to me!' they yell.

'Stewie, Stewie, Stewie!'

'Buddha, Buddha, Buddhaaaaaa!!!!!!'

The cacophony of noise increases. The thud of heavy boots on balls contributes to the din of the players' voices. Footballs fly up and out through the whiteness, then gracefully arc, disappear back where they came. The sound is reminiscent of pop-corn, but ten times louder.

'Okay youse blokes listen up…' the voice of the coach bellows out like a fog horn on a grounded ship, summoning his men to order, to listen. The footballs stay out of the stratosphere while the coach speaks to his team - respect is instinctively owed to the coach. He gives instructions to the warriors of the game.

With a united yell of 'Yeah!' and 'C'mon guys!' they break up, spreading across the soggy oval.

On such a cold night the coach's breath is streaming out of his mouth, making him seem like a fiery dragon as he urges them to run harder and harder. He is in command as they sprint and rigorously throw themselves into ball-handling exercises.

Frantic shouts of 'Macca! Macca! Macca! Here to me! To me...' rise above the foggy barrier as play gets underway. The ghostly hails, combined with the sound of shrill whistles and seagull cries, rise and fall, like the ground swell of an ocean wave.

Once more footballs are booted high, with a thudding sound up into the evening sky. They dip and weave among the Silver gulls, like un-natural birds diving in a sea of white.

The overhead lights catch on the white feathers of the sea birds and the red leather of the balls, casting eerie shadows onto the foggy veil below. Unlike the birds, gravity has a say in how long the footballs can stay above the clouds, dragging them down to earth. Back into the arms of the spectre who kicked it.

Finally, after the crescendo has peaked, a feeling of testosterone-fuelled happiness filters from the players. The coach seems pleased by the good work the lads have done tonight. He congratulates them and informs them they 'are gonna murder the opposition on Saturday'. A resounding cheer and numerous calls of 'YEAH!!' from the players confirm his opinion of their ability to effectively destroy their opponents on the week-end.

The noises and unseen voices become subdued murmurs, as the pack moves away from the ground and into the club rooms, leaving the gulls to fly helplessly around the light towers. With a flick of a switch, somewhere in the Bonbeach Footy Club Rooms, the lights turn off, gradually powering down, leaving the bewildered Silver gulls floundering in the sudden darkness.

A deafening silence passes over the oval with the departure of the urban warriors, leaving winter to cover itself with a blanket of fog, close his eyes, and settle down for the night.

Not again! I couldn't believe it! Honestly what had I done in a former life??

Let me start at the beginning. I sometimes rent a room out, or two or three. It's part of my poverty management plan. I had to let my financial manager go, (oh alright, I never had one). Because I had my mother with me a couple of times to convalesce I hadn't had someone renting for a while so I accepted two guys who were working nearby and commuting interstate. I don't have a big house, but I've turned the lounge room into a bedsit.

Matthew, tenant/boarder No. 2 was a tall well built guy in his mid twenties with some really impressive looking tattoos, but a thoroughly gentle nature. He was easy going and relaxed, until... He arrived back from work one afternoon and sought me out while I was watering the garden.

'Do you know the phone number for the local police?' he asked, his eyes slits of steel.

I rattled it off quickly. His eyebrows rose at my instant reply. I shrugged. He hurried off to phone the cops. After he'd done that he came to chat, which loosely translated, meant turn the air blue about 'people' who had nothing better to do than thieve from hardworking men. And they were hardworking; putting in twelve hour days, for eleven days straight, before having three days off. The thieves had picked the wrong guy on the wrong day. Suffice it to say that in recent times, 'life had been a bitch'. Well there was something about a bitch in there...

They had taken his GPS and about $500 worth of electronic gear he'd just bought. He had a mutter to his mates, then had a mutter to me. I told him about my episodes with 'Vandals and thieves' (see related stories) and I confided the name and location of the 'usual suspect'. I told him of the ongoing problems, electricity turned off, TV connections unplugged, bolts taken out, security lights broken, things stolen – the list seemed endless.

'Mmm,' said Matthew, 'might do a random walk around the neighbourhood, visit a few people. I'll see if anyone saw anything—and visit that kid.'

Now one doesn't offer advice to grown men renting rooms, but in the interest of the success of his mission I casually suggested he might have less trouble 'making his point' if his tattoos were clearly visible. To my surprise he went and changed into a muscle shirt. Off he went, his lithe 6 foot frame ramrod straight and determined. He was wearing his thin sunglasses. Only a single-celled amoeba would have missed his attitude. He had a casual chat with the neighbours on both sides, and across the road, and then he was out of sight. I went inside—he didn't need me staring after him, like a nervous puppy. He was back soon.

'Yeah, that kid's the one alright. Looked as guilty as sin as soon he opened the door.' Matthew went on to relate the rest of the conversation that had me gaping. Being around teenage boys and young men, I thought I'd heard everything. Apparently not.

'I told the little shit I'd be back in 30 minutes for my stuff and if it wasn't there I would &#*% him. I told him, 'I know people who know people' and if he wanted a peaceful life he'd leave this house alone for the rest of his miserable life.'

Oh crap, I thought. I'd been calm up to this point, but then my mind ran off to the reprisals I might suffer when these guys left. There were two men staying with a third guy arriving the next day on the same contract job. What then for me? What if I got it wrong? I would have chewed my nails, but I had none left. I said nothing, deciding to keep to myself for the designated 30 minutes. I nervously went back to watering. I was just washing up when Matthew came back through the door.

He was loaded up with all of his stolen stuff. I'm not often speechless, general anaesthetic being the only proven time, but that day my jaw was on the floor. Everything was in its original boxes and plastic bags.

'I suppose you're going to tell me you even got the receipts,' I said, when I found my voice.

'Better than that,' he said, lifting the lid of the cardboard box back to reveal some writing.

'I got the little creep to get a pen and write down the name of his friend and accomplice.'

My eyes were like saucers and his friend, the other boarder Deakin, came to the scene equally stunned. There on the box lid, was not only a name, but an address and phone number.

'I don't think the cops get this kind of result,' I mumbled.

'Still got to 'visit' the other prick,' said Matthew.

'Oh,' was all I could manage.

I wasn't privy to the details of the other visit—and quite frankly just wanted to lie down. A man's world belonged to a man, not a wuss like me.

Matthew and Deakin's friend, Danno arrived the next day. He had a huge double cabin ute with logos and bull bars and other stuff—forgive me for the lack of information—I'm a girl. This guy was older and tougher, and sported even more impressive 'tatts'. The guys had a barbeque at the back, sat me down with a beer and recounted the story. With my head already swimming, I was glad for the beer. Matthew and Danno went for a drive. Danno's arrival couldn't have been timed better. After Matthew's subtle statement that 'he knew people who knew people' it must have looked like the 'big boss from out of town' had arrived.

Matthew and Danno arrived back to say they'd visited the culprits again because the security codes for Matthew's gear was missing.

'I think we scared the crap out of the whole family,' said Matthew.

'Certainly made the father shit himself,' said Danno.

I didn't know how much more excitement I could take. The thought that, for once, someone bigger was on my side was strangely exhilarating. Terrifying, but definitely exhilarating. I tried to turn off the side of my brain worrying how it could all go terribly wrong, and enjoy the moment.

'I'm living in 'Underbelly', only on the right side,' I exclaimed. They all grinned.

The next day I opened the door to a strange man. He appeared to be trembling slightly. He introduced himself as the father of one of the boys. He wanted to know if I could ask Matthew to phone him and handed me his mobile number. Slightly emboldened by having 'back up' for the first time in history I announced that it 'wasn't my business', but I didn't think Matthew would want to waste valuable mobile phone time on someone who'd already ripped him off.

'Why don't you come back when they're home?' I suggested helpfully.

He appeared to put this idea on a par with being alone with a hungry crocodile and quickly left.

If the boarders were chuffed when I referred to them as 'The Underbelly Crew', they didn't show it. I wondered how it would be when they left. To my astonishment not a leaf on a tree was touched.

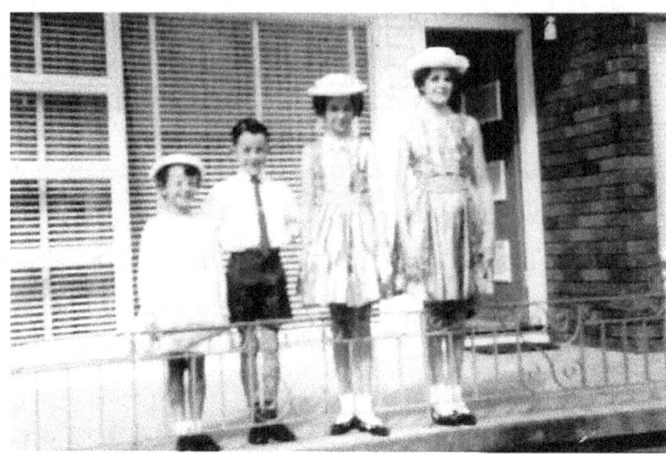

It was the same routine every week – rain, hail or shine. I would wake up to the gentle prodding of my Dad as he tried to get me out of bed around 7am.

'Time to get moving,' he'd say, as he continued on his rounds to wake up my two sisters and my brother in the same manner. Mum would already be in the kitchen making the porridge, setting the table. It was the 1960's and it was Sunday – the best day of the week. Sunday was 'Church Day'.

We'd gather around the breakfast table and as soon as Dad said Grace we would get stuck into our porridge, Weet-Bix with warm milk, or Cornflakes, and our vegemite toast. I can still remember the days we got to open a *new* cereal box. There would be special cards to collect, or a small plastic toy wrapped (hygienically) in a cellophane packet. All the kids at school collected them and sometimes you got to swap with someone who had duplicates they were keen to exchange.

Once breakfast was over and done with we would get dressed in our 'Sunday clothes'. We loved our Sunday clothes! Among these beautiful outfits would be the ones that Grandma had made for us to wear to the annual Sunday School Anniversary. Sometimes they had net or cotton petticoats that Mum would starch the day before so that our frocks would stick out from the waist. We had special Sunday shoes and hats, and sometimes gloves as well. My older sister and I always had dresses that were identical in style and fabric, but different in colour. My brother always wore grey shorts, white shirt and a tie.

In the early 60's we didn't own a car so our family of 6 would walk to Church. We lived in

Wiley Park and our church, Lakemba Baptist Church was in the next suburb, so it would take us about 30 – 40 mins to do the trip. We were all so grateful when Grandpa bought his first FJ Holden and passed his old Morris Oxford on to us. We felt so 'important' driving to Church!

We'd arrive at Church in time for Sunday School at 9.30am and then into the 11am Church service with the 'grown ups'. Our family filled an entire wooden pew. I remember my brother occasionally receiving the 'razor strap' when we got home for being naughty during the service! After Church I was sometimes allowed to go to my friend Margaret's home for lunch. Her mother insisted we don aprons so as not to spoil our Sunday Clothes while eating or playing afterwards.

At around 3pm we children would walk back to Church for Christian Endeavour. This was a kind of Kid's Club, where we would learn memory verses and play Bible games. Once a year we would sit for our Scripture Exams. I always did well and I remember feeling proud of myself at each Sunday School Anniversary when prizes were awarded to the children who had done well in their exams! CE (as it was affectionately known) was partly run by the children ourselves and supervised by adults. We took turns being President, Secretary and Treasurer. It was a lot of fun.

Then it was back home, get stuck into some dinner, and back to Church for the 7.30pm night service. Sometimes we might have a 'visiting speaker' – usually a missionary from Africa. I would listen, spellbound, as the speaker told of jungles and head-hunters, and showed slides of smiling dark faces (occasionally I would blush when shots of half naked women would come up!). Even though I knew the importance of sharing God's love with these people I earnestly prayed that God would never ask me to go to Africa!

Although our Sundays were busy, we never tired of our Church activity. I still remember the excitement of boarding the Church bus to go on Sunday School picnics which took place on Saturdays. All the kids were given an orange, a cream bun and a white paper bag of lollies. Mums and Dads came along too and join in the games – egg and spoon races, sack races, wheelbarrow races and the like. We would usually fall asleep on the trip home – tired and sunburnt, but happy and content.

Then there was Girls' Brigade (GB)– similar to Girl Guides – on a Friday night. I loved GB too – we would do marching drill etc, but what I loved most was the craft activities. There were badges to be earned for various accomplishments, and our mothers would sew them on to the sleeves of our GB uniforms. And the regular Sunday Church Fellowship lunches when each family would bring lunch to share in the Church Hall after the service: lots of egg sandwiches, scones and pikelets with jam and cream, and cordial. Also lots of fun and games running around the Church grounds and lots of laughter! Sunday life wasn't just about Church though – it was about Family as well.

After we got our first car, we would sometimes miss CE meetings on a Sunday afternoon and drive over to Homebush to see Grandma and Grandpa. We loved Grandma and Grandpa! And they loved us. Grandma would often patiently sit beside me on the piano seat and teach me to play duets with her. Grandpa would love to tease and tickle us with his rough carpenter's hands. Sometimes we kids would help out with bottling the peaches by collecting them from the tree in the back yard, or helping Grandpa peel them (he would use a knife; we were only allowed to use the potato peeler). Then Grandma and Mum would put them in the pot for stewing. I can still smell that sweet aroma of stewing peaches while I pen this memory! And there's something about the taste of home-stewed peaches that cannot be matched by the canned variety I buy these days.

I can remember times when went to Church with Grandma and Grandpa. They attended Belvoir St. Baptist Church in the city. I remember this being an old, dark church with large stain-glassed windows. After the service we would all enjoy Fellowship Lunch together and then a team of us would go into Redfern and do 'door-to-door'. This meant knocking on the doors of houses and inviting children to come to the park for some fun and Sunday School activities. The kids would come in droves! Someone would play an accordion and we would sing choruses with great gusto. Someone else would use a flannel board to relate a Bible story. After an hour or so we'd head back to church, share some dinner, attend the night service and then finally drive home. A long day – but a good one!

On other Sunday afternoons we might drive to Marrickville to spend time with a couple of Dad's maiden aunts. While Dad and Mum chatted with Aunty Clarice and Aunty Marj, we kids would go exploring their mysteriously dark house, or watch their black and white TV (we didn't have one) and eat Minties or Pascals fruit lollies from the cutglass dish on the mantelpiece. Dad was always keen to make sure his parents and these aunts were doing ok.

Yes, Sunday was, for me growing up in the 60's, the best day of the week. Church was central to our life as a family. And Family was central to Church life. We shared wonderful friendships and the ups and downs of life with other great families. Dad and Mum made sure our Christian faith was alive and real in each of our lives. I'm so grateful for the wonderful foundations laid in my life through those early childhood Church years.

In fact, Church and my Christian faith has always been central to my life. Today my husband and I pastor a great little Church of our own.

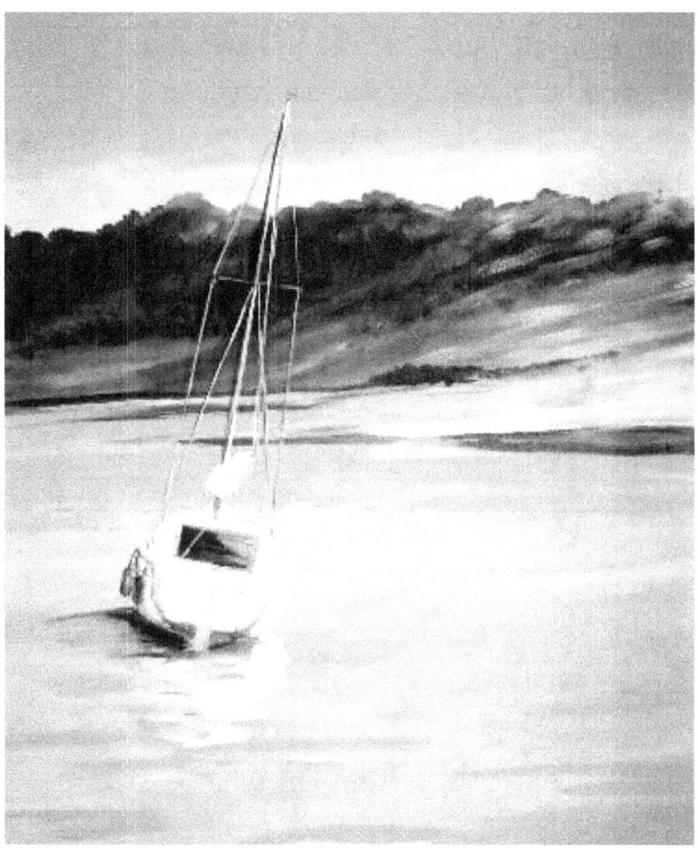

Friggadig sat on her trailer in the driveway ready to go.

Dave and his mates were heading away for the Australia Day long week-end. Like them, I enjoy camping and getting away from the maddening boredom of suburbia. So, I was invited to come along and join him sailing.

A tent, sleeping bags, food and alcoholic beverages, enough to last two days, were flung,- in an orderly fashion of course - into the back of Dave's 1973 Holden HQ Premier Station wagon. We also packed our wetsuits, buoyancy vest and harnesses as *Friggadig* was - according to Dave- not a 'particularly dry boat'.

In 1985, my understanding of sailing was limited to say the least. I'd never been sailing before. My 'experience' of sailing was limited to watching it. I had seen Australia Two defeat the Americans in the 1983 America's Cup on T.V. Even then I'd watched the outcome on a telly in a shop window, as I was passing on my way to do more important things.

The window was surrounded by other curious bystanders. I had to ask the person standing beside me what all the fuss was about - such was the extent of my involvement with boats. The next thing I knew, our Prime Minister Bob Hawke, was enthusiastically telling us our 'bosses were mugs if they didn't give us the day off work'. Hoorah for sailing!

According to me, *Friggadig* was a yellow dinghy. It was actually a 12.5 foot intermediate sailing dinghy made with the stitch and glue plywood method. Its weight was approximately 50kg with a beam of 1.43m, and was called 125 after its overall imperial length. But I didn't know any of this at the time.

Waranga Basin in Northern Victoria was our week-end destination. This body of water is a holding basin for the irrigation system which carries water for the dry parched northern part of the state. In 1985 it was 'quite full'. Well, full enough for us to sail on apparently.

After setting up our camping site we hopped into our wetsuits and took *Friggadig* down to the water's edge. Dave, being the expert at the whole sailing thing, attached the stays, then put up the mast. I had no idea which bit of wire went where and, to my uneducated –in the way of all things nautical - eye, it looked like a very complicated mess indeed.

Dave attached and tied things onto the boat.

'What are those wires for?' I asked.

'So the mast doesn't fall down,' was Dave's reply as he attached and hoisted the sails.

'Oh, I see,' I said. But I didn't. Help me now, I thought.

The whole contraption looked very flimsy; hardly big enough to contain both of us.

'It doesn't look very stable,' I mumbled as he helped me do up the harness I had slipped on over my wetsuit.

'It'll be fine. I'll be there to give you a 'chop out' if you need it,' he assured me. I had reservations about THAT statement!

Dave gave me a quick run-down on how the trapeze worked, instructed me on how the jib sheets ran and what to do with them. Seriously, I thought, aren't sheets what you lie on in bed?

Brimming with something between abject terror and excitement, we boarded *Friggadig* - very tentatively. Once we were seated, Dave took hold of the tiller, pulled in the main sheet, shoved the centreboard into the slot in the little casing that protruded above the floor of the boat. Away we went, out into the middle of the basin. Wow what a rush!

The wind was a gentle 10-15 knot breeze creating rippled waves and *Friggadig* skipped like a pebble across the surface of the water. We had our feet hooked under the straps on the deck and our bums hanging over the gunwale keeping her hull as level as possible. Apparently this is called 'hiking out'.

'If you want to get out on the trapeze…' Dave called out as the boat suddenly heeled with an on-coming gust '...*now would be a good time…*'

I was feeling very brave, or perhaps crazy under the exciting spell of going like the stink. I grabbed the trapeze wire, fastened it to the hook on my harness, pushed myself up onto my feet, then up and out onto the gunwale – literally hanging in the breeze. Not a bad effort for a first timer, I thought.

'Think heavy!' Dave yelled from his place at the tiller, as the boat heeled further up on its side with the stiffening breeze.

All 49 kilos of me was hanging out from the boat as far as physically possible, suspended on a wire out in the air and thinking heavy thoughts. The next thing I knew, we hit a bumpy wave and my harness was released from the trapeze. With a 49 kilo gram splash, I was in the drink.

There was *Friggadig* sailing off into the distance. The loss of my weight on the trapeze hadn't even caused her to stop or fall over. So much for 'thinking heavy'.

It took Dave a while to turn the boat to come back and retrieve me from the water. We continued sailing that day and for the rest of the week-end.I was hooked on sailing.

('Friggadig – Jennifer Goard)

Troy Berrier revved the motor and turned for a glance at the crowd behind him. Even through the insulation of his helmet he could hear them screaming themselves hoarse. Bodies swarmed and bashed up against each other like overcharged electrons. Their energy made him ten times stronger and more flexible. The bike beneath him trembled.

He would do the Death Spin.

Don't go too hard, he told himself. *She wants more throttle, but she's just greedy. I still want her in one piece when I hit the downramp. I need a bit more, but only a bit. That much.*

He took the kicker dead-centre. First up was a Saran Wrap, his legs moving perfectly around the handlebars. Another perfect take-off, and this time he nailed a Kiss of Death. His next trick was a Double-Grab Indian air.

He took the kicker again. Every bone and muscle and nerve in his body knew before he even did the trick, he would land it spot-on. He stretched out above the hovering bike, his body straight and stiff. Then in a neat, precise move, he spun in the air, a 360 degree torpedo above the motorbike, spotting the fuel cap below him like a dancer. He found the handlebars and returned to the ground.

The noise from the crowd was deafening. The chain link fence swayed drunkenly, finally submitting to the force behind it. Troy laughed as the crowd rushed up to greet him.

With this event over, Troy had the MX-Stream games to concentrate on. Sean, his coach, had him focused, training hard and getting fit and strong enough for it.

Sean was elated with Troy's progress. He had never seen him jump so well. Troy's body had responded to the diet Sean had laid out for him. Consistent training had built Troy into a wall of solid muscle.

'All right,' Sean said, as Troy pulled up. 'We've got a week to go before MX-Stream. I want you to try something different this time. I want you to take a week off. You're not going to touch a bike at all, until the practice session at the games. Not even your road bike. Not even your mate's bike. If you need to go somewhere, get your parents to drive you. Also, we don't train. Don't run, don't lift a weight - don't do anything - for that whole week. I just want you to rest, and not think about the games until maybe Thursday.'

Troy grinned. 'Does that mean that partying is back on the agenda, then?'

Sean laughed. 'What do y'think? After these games, you're a free man, Troy. Until then, no!'

Sean was nervous about these games. This was like playing at the home ground. Everyone would be pumped. And added to the excitement there would be a film crew scouting for talent for a movie with Justin Warner. Justin was a legend. Sean was sure Troy would perform well, and it would be icing on the cake for him to star in a motocross movie. There was a lot at stake.

Troy beamed the grin he'd been wearing for the past two weeks. 'Don't worry, Sean. If they wanna beat me, they're gonna have to fit their bikes with wings.'

'Yeah, I believe you. Just remember, no training. I'm serious Troy.'

'Okay, but that's going to kill me. Can I bring a couple of people to the MX?'

'You can bring the whole town if you want.'

Troy grinned. 'I better get on the phone, then.'

The first call was to Shelley. She was his biggest fan, as well as being a top friend. She'd reserved her place months ago.

I missed Sydney last year, there's no way I'm missing it this year, she'd said.

'You still right for the weekend?' he asked.

'Troy, there's no way on Earth I am gonna miss these games, 'cause I know you're gonna be magic!'

He chuckled. He didn't need a crowd of thousands. Shelley did just as good a job at pumping him up all by herself. 'I'll try, that's for sure, Shel,' he said. 'It's all set. If you wanna come with us, we're out of here at 4.00 am.'

'No probs. Kiara wants to come too. Will there be room for her?'

'Sure thing.'

Saturday morning emerged in a shroud of mist, stabbed by the white light of a streetlight. The girls, rugged up and still half-asleep, were standing around, watching the goings on as the men loaded bikes and equipment.

Troy was jumping out of his skin. His father, David Berrier, was ready with the car and trailer loaded with the bikes. He was on time, as always. Troy was grateful for his parent's support.

The girls climbed into the back of the car, and were both asleep by the time they were on the freeway. Troy hadn't stopped talking since he'd closed the passenger side door. David smiled. Troy was really pumped. By the time they pulled into the showground, he'd grated his father's nerves back to the bone.

'What d'ya need me to do for ya, Dad?'

'I need you to take the girls and get out of my sight for an hour or two,' David replied, grinning.

Troy laughed. 'Yeah, no worries.'

The tension would build as show time came, but now it was time for a chat and catch-up. He would take the girls and look for his friend, and fellow competitor, Seth. Seth was a top bloke and they'd competed at the same events for years.

Practice went well. Sean's words before Troy went out were stern, 'Don't go out there and blast it, Troy. I know you're a coiled spring at the moment, but conserve your energy. Store as much of it as you can.'

Troy nodded. He used the practice session just to gauge what he was up against in terms of the kickers. No one was showing anyone else anything. Any onlooker would have thought they had stumbled into the under-10 division with all the lame whips everyone was throwing around.

Tension slowly seeped into the atmosphere. It was palpable. He had to concentrate more on channelling the rising energy inside. The crowd was really pumped tonight. Something special was going to happen, and they knew it. It took ages for the finals to come around. When they did, Troy was ready.

Seth finished his set. He had nailed it. He pulled up beside Troy and ripped off his helmet. 'It's singin' out there, but just try and keep off the left side of that second down-ramp. I think John musta dropped some oil when he had that off in the heat.'

Troy nodded, touching Seth's outstretched knuckle with his own. 'Thanks.' He took his gloves from Shelley who was standing nearby.

'Good luck,' she said, as she handed him his helmet.

He leaned over and gave her a kiss on the cheek. 'Thanks, Shel.'

Kiara came running up to stand next to Shelley. With the roar of the crowd in the background, she could only mouth the words, 'good luck,' to him as he revved the motorbike hard. He took off towards the ramp. Finally allowed to release all of this stored energy his body sang with joy.

The crowd roared approvingly at his no-handed catwalk. He got six steps in before he returned the bike to land. This was the time he could do anything and get away with it. They had hardly gotten over roaring their approval at his first trick before he was up again, his kiss of death so vertical he almost tipped himself over the front of the bike.

They weren't prepared for the combo, and screamed in delight at witnessing the new trick. He slowed slightly, getting himself together. Giving the bike an injection of power he hit the kicker again. His position was perfect.

The crowd were on their feet by the time he had landed the Death Spin. The earth shook from the waves of sound and movement, a seething mass of joy and appreciation of his efforts. He pulled up. He had nailed it.

In the pit area, Troy took off his gloves, goggles and helmet and gave them to Sean. Sean grabbed Troy in a congratulatory hug. 'That was magic, Troy! Come and meet Justin Warner's cameraman. He's taken some great photos and wants to show them to you. I think he's seriously impressed. If you're lucky you won't just take a trophy home tonight, you might get a role in Justin's movie.'

Troy was stunned when he saw the photos. There was a beautiful shot of him mid Death Spin. The lights of the stadium, and a thousand flashbulbs frozen in the shot, made him look as though he was flying through stars.

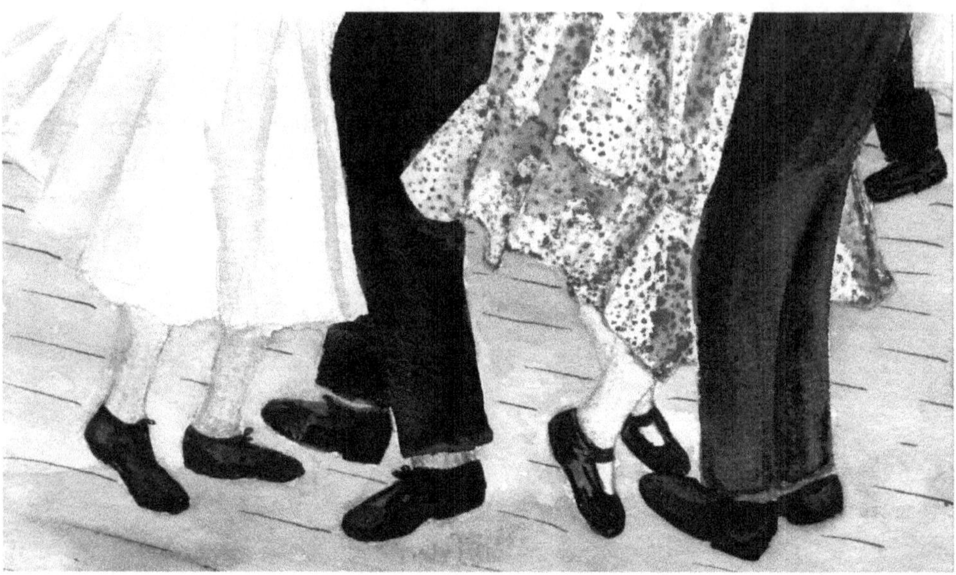

There was a scramble for the cars, but eventually everybody arrived at the hotel entrance, although rather wet.

Kitty's crinoline of pink satin, which had stood out from the hips, now clung around her ankles and made her resemble a hot air balloon. Her hair had gone from bouffant to flat with the flowered wreath looking quite unfortunate. The best man had provided another girl with his jacket for protection, leaving Kitty to fend for herself. He had quite forgotten one of his jobs was to look after the bridesmaid. Fortunately, somebody had offered their golf umbrella to protect the happy couple and they had arrived without any mishap.

Mr and Mrs Brandt, the elder, were long-faced; they were not pleased with how things were turning out. This would not have happened in South Australia, they might get rain occasionally but it was always at the right time. The weather would not dare to misbehave in their home state.

Mrs Dixon was wringing her hands as well as the part of her suit was soaking wet. How could this have happened to spoil things on her daughter's big day? What was wrong with the weather bureau, that they could never get things right? It was said that rain on the wedding day foretold bad times ahead. But she did not for a moment believe all these old wives tales and superstitions!

The manager of the hotel made his condolences about the weather and offered one of the smaller bedrooms for the guests to use if they wished to freshen up. Mr Dixon was pleased about that, but felt he must mention the cost not be added to the bill. The manager assured him that all would be well; it would be his personal contribution to the festivities.

After the guests had shaken hands with Marian and Ivor and given their best wishes, most of them feeling quite awkward with this unaccustomed ceremony, they were ushered into the splendid ballroom which was far and away too large for the number assembled. There, they were offered drinks and they stood around in uncomfortable small groups, trying to find something to talk about.

With the photograph session over at last, Marian and Ivor were led in by the Maitre d'hotel resplendent in full evening dress.

'Ladies and gentlemen may I present to you, Mr and Mrs Ivor Brandt,' he announced in his booming voice.

They took their indicated places at the beautifully silver-set, orchid-strewn table. Kitty was seated beside Marian with Bob, the best man, next to her. Kitty leaned as close as she dare, with her knees brushing his.

Marian, although feeling slightly out of her depth at the sumptuousness of the surroundings, drew herself up to sit proudly. She was now Mrs Ivor Brandt, a 'somebody'; her own woman, at last.

Ivor felt overwhelmed with the overly decorated palace and would have preferred to spend his time in the local with Bob. He didn't hold with all this stuff and nonsense some people went on with.

Bob was looking across the room to ascertain where a certain girl was sitting at one of the round tables. He wished he could sit with her, but hoped to make a play for her later, given the opportunity. He caught her eye and winked. I wonder who she is, he thought. Somebody said her name was Janelle; nice name. Perhaps she's a relative, a cousin or something. This suit I hired isn't all that comfortable, but at least Ivor took notice of what I suggested and insisted on us both wearing lounge suits; none of that nonsense of tails and top hats! I can just imagine what his ma-in-law said when he told her, in no uncertain terms, that he was not going to get himself up into a monkey suit. A right old battleaxe she looks. I bet she gets her own way all the time. This place is really something, but I'd really rather be down at the local with the guys. I hope Ivor is not going to opt out of the group now he's married. Give him a couple of weeks after the honeymoon to appear willing; so his bride can't complain, then we'll get him back to the pub. I never figured Ivor as the marrying type. He's always had any girl he fancied, what's so special about this one, that he had to marry her?

Now that blonde chick over there, she looks like she could be a goer. And she's got all the attributes. Yer never know yer luck; where yer gonna meet someone like that. I'm glad now that Ivor asked me to be best man. How long have we been cobbers? Two years since I joined the firm, yeah. This stupid bridesmaid keeps leaning all over me. Can't she sit up straight?

At last an army of waiters started to serve food and wine. Now the guests relaxed sufficiently to partake of the food and wine that was placed before them, but conversation was still rather stilted. Both Mr and Mrs Brandt senior sniffed at the choice of a soup or entrée, disliking both. Mrs Brandt was tempted to pick up the main course of a piece of chicken as it arrived, to see what was hidden beneath, and sniffed again at the choice of vegetables. If she had been consulted she would have chosen something other than Brussels sprouts and pumpkin!

Denise Dixon sat very upright, she had been instrumental in choosing the dishes and she was darned if she was not going to enjoy every one, in spite of it playing havoc with her figure! She cast a beaming smile around the room and took another swig of wine.

Seated at the end of the horseshoe shaped table Michael found it hard to suppress a grin. Every time his mother turned her head the ridiculous hat nearly knocked out her neighbour's eye. But since the person sitting next to her was Stephan Brandt, Michael felt no sympathy for the man.

Michael had, when he first met the Brandts, tried to be friendly and say something to the effect that he was pleased to welcome them to this great city. The Brandts had glared ferociously at him in reply and had done their best to ignore him since.

I think, Marian, you are welcome to your new Mother and Father-in law, he thought. At least I will not have to meet up with them in the future; it will be Marian's problem to deal with them. But I do wish mother wouldn't put on airs and graces. It really is a laugh how she pretends she is used to all this opulence. Of course, Dad is having the time of his life. I should think he has invited enough of his business cronies to help him along for the next twelve months. Uncle Al looks as if he's having a good time but Auntie Joan looks like she is eating sour lemons.

I'm glad Marian put her foot down about the seating. I know I have to sit at the top table, but my girl-friend would have hated it. Anyway, Marian let me ask her best mate to come too and they seem to be enjoying themselves sitting with Mum's youngest sister. I'm pleased about that. She's usually a jolly sort of person. She and Cynthia would have a similar sort of sense of humour. There are just a few younger people here; but I get really cheesed off with the oldies. They just don't understand us at all. Just listen to that stupid music the group is playing, I'll bet they would rather be playing rock.

Marian sat rigidly. She knew her mother had been drinking steadily and hoped she would not make a fool of herself before the day was out. She is not used to wine; it is only about once a week that dad pours a drink for her, on Saturday evenings. I don't know why that is. Perhaps that's the night they plan to have sex. At least Dad stays home on weekends, not like Jeanie's father.

I'm pleased I sent an invitation to Jeanie. There she is, sitting with the other girls from the office. So far they don't seem to have made any contact with anybody else. I suppose we should have invited more young men. But even Michael didn't want to put many names on the list. And with Dad limiting the number of guests, it became a bit difficult. But still, I am glad I asked the girls from work. They don't get asked out much. You'd think some of them would get lots of invites; those on the front counter anyway. After all they are meeting the public all the time. But fortunately that's not my job. It will be good having a couple of weeks off. Our supervisor went to Bali for her honeymoon, lucky her!

But our motel by the sea looks pretty good in the brochures. I wonder if I will like married life. I'm not sure about the bedroom part. And how is Ivor going to cope with all these little buttons down my back? I wish now I had chosen the strapless dress, but this is nice. It does show off my boobs without being too immodest. I wish Mum hadn't given me this present. What am I going to do with a tiara after this? I wonder why mothers, my mother anyway, want to do so many things for weddings? Is it because they had such a simple one themselves, because they had no money? Well, we haven't got much either. It's just as well Dad was prepared to cough up for the whole thing. This place is something else. I suppose I will look back on it all and I will remember all these trappings and be pleased about it.

I hope the photos turn out all right. That photographer is getting a lot of pictures; he seems to be taking one of everybody here. I hope we don't have to pay for all of them. Whatever is Dad talking about? Did I just hear him say that he is going to miss me being around? What a load of rubbish. For one thing he is nearly always in his factory or some meeting or other; anyway, he has always been more interested in what Michael is up to, rather than what I do.

Oh no! I just heard him say, 'today the chance of young people finding happiness through marriage is almost impossible.' That's nice, that is! Does he think Ivor and I are not going to be happy! Of course we'll be happy. I think Mum should give him a good kick under the table, but she just has a silly look on her face. There he is again, 'The rise of our divorce rate is frightening.' Dad you'd better be careful!

Oh dear, now he is spouting statistics about the divorce rate. How inappropriate! If Mum is not going to stop him I will! There, that should shut him up for a while.

Ed Dixon thought his speech was going well, until his daughter kicked him under the table and he let out a yelp. After that he just mumbled and lost the thread of what he was going to say, but people applauded anyway so he sat down.

Then it was the turn of the best man to say something nice about the bridesmaid. He looked steadily at the girl, held his champagne glass up and proposed a toast – 'to girls everywhere.' Then he remembered his job and said, 'um – to the bridesmaid.'

Kitty shifted herself happily, thinking, he noticed me, he likes me, just wait until we get dancing; he'll like me even more then! Her face wore a foolish grin.

The cake was cut; the bride and groom toasted each other, each silently wishing - for different reasons - that this shindig was ending.

Speeches over, the little band started playing again; the bridal waltz consisted of a selection of songs from the 1950s and even earlier. Mrs Dixon prodded Ivor and with her eyes, indicated he lead Marian to the floor to start the dancing.

Ivor hadn't the slightest idea that was expected of him and sat silently until he was prodded on the other side by his bride. Then he got to his feet at the same time as Marian, who felt they had delayed long enough and was about to grab at his sleeve to pull him on to the floor. Ivor's hand was limp on her back, his arm flopped badly and his feet were everywhere, including on Marian's oyster satin shoes. Marian was disappointed. She hadn't expected her beloved was anything but a superb dancer.

Disappointed too, was her bridesmaid who had waited and waited, to be asked by the best man. Finally she decided she was not prepared to wait any longer to be asked, so she grabbed his hand and dragged him, reluctantly, to the floor. His efforts were even worse than the bridegroom's. People could see that as a pair these two men were not even fit for a soccer field.

Both Marian and Kitty, upset at this outcome, went straight to the powder room at the end of the bridal waltz; it was an excuse to get away from the staring faces of the guests. There they made small talk about nothing and spent a long time doing their faces.

Denise Dixon, seeing them go, decided to follow but was waylaid by Joan, her sister-in-law. When she finally got away she went into the wrong restroom and only realised her mistake when a man came out of one of the cubicles zipping up his fly. She let out a scream which brought several more men running in to enquire what the fuss was about. By this time her hat was decidedly awry and her tight skirt had crept up to reveal fat knees. Far from being the image she had hoped to project today, she was slightly tipsy and about to collapse in a heap.

One of the men put his arm about her waist and led her away to be met outside the door by Mrs Brandt, also on her way to the ladies room. The look on her face pronounced Denise as a loose woman indeed and not someone she should 'know'!

Michael Dixon, watching the dancers, hoped he would not have this chore as another of his duties, when his father stood beside him, saying, 'You look a little lost, son.'

'Weddings are for girls, Dad.'

'You'll be having one of your own some day.'

'You reckon?'

'Why not? There's lots of nice girls.'

Michael laughed. 'Yeah, 'he said.

'Why aren't you dancing, Michael?' his father asked.

'Oh Dad, this is not for me. I am not a bit interested in all this.'

'Go on, ask that pretty girl over there. We went to all the trouble to get the band to play music you like, now dance!'

Michael sighed. Not all the music was really to his taste, even when the small group had switched to some more up-to-date songs. But he said, 'Which girl are you talking about Dad?'

'That long-haired brunette, she looks like a nice girl. I could go for her myself.'

'Then it's just as well you don't, she is my friend. And yes, Cynthia is a nice girl.'

'Sorry son. So you do have a girlfriend? '

'Not really a girl-friend, just a friend.'

'Well, you'd better get going, ask her to dance or someone else will snap her up.'

Michael sighed again, but he did elbow his way towards Cynthia and suggest they attack the floor together. Since it was a real Rock'n'Roll number they did not have to spend time with their arms around each other, but could do their own jigging and jiving well apart. At the end Michael led her to the bar, where he intended to spend the rest of the evening. But after a while, Cynthia suggested that they decorate the bridal car, so they vanished into the car park with a few more of the young people.

Penny, one of the cousins, was sent to find out where the bride had hidden. People were beginning to notice that she was absent and wondered if she was ill. It did not take long to find Marian, but instead of collecting Penny, she joined in the conversation. It was all about the various assets of different boys that Kitty had hoped to get to know. 'Do you think Brad is better than Bob?' she asked the others.

'I don't really know Brad, or Bob, come to that,' Marian said. 'I have met them, of course, but I didn't really form an opinion.'

'Do you think Bob likes me?' Kitty went on, 'I mean, enough to ask me to go out with him.'

Marian was now in a quandary. From what she had seen of Bob's behaviour that evening, it was unlikely that he would ever ask Kitty to go out with him. Nor, she thought, would Kitty be wise to go with him, even if he should ask her. Poor Kitty, she was breaking her neck to find a boyfriend. 'What do you think, Penny?' she asked her cousin.

Penny tossed her head. 'I wouldn't give two bob for either of them,' she said. 'They've both got tickets on themselves.' Penny said she would invite Kitty to a party to meet a few friends of hers the following week which cheered the girl up no end.

When Marian, Kitty and Penny, finally emerged from the powder room it was to find a noisy brawl in progress.

On enquiry they were told that Bob, the best man, had followed Janelle, into the bedroom reserved for the guests, and there he had attempted to climb on top of her as she sat on the bed. She had screamed and two of the other male guests had rushed in, pulled him off and were now in the process of 'teaching the bastard a lesson'. It took no time for a few others to join in, and some old scores appeared to be settled. The band played a Rolling Stones number loudly in an effort to cover the noise of the melee. The hotel manager was soon on the scene accompanied by two large bouncers. The fight was quickly subdued. the manager had a quiet word with Mr Dixon.

Ed Dixon suggested the going-away car be brought around immediately. He had noticed Ivor starting to sway on his feet. It would not do for the bridegroom to go straight to sleep on his first night.

Marian threw her bouquet which hit her Auntie Joan in the mouth, making her expression even more sour than before.

Among cries of 'good luck' and some other vulgar or bawdy remarks the car took off for the honeymooner's first night, to the rattling of tin cans. At last, around midnight, Ivor and Marian arrived at their motel and had to awaken the proprietor. He had expected them two hours earlier and as they had not arrived by 10pm had gone to bed. He received a shock when he saw Marian in her wedding dress. Not realising it was a honeymoon couple he had reserved a tiny unit, with two single beds as well as the double. There was hardly enough room to turn around; but he assured them he would give them a better room, when next they came to his establishment.

Marian was so tired all she wanted was to flop down on one of the beds, she didn't much care which one. However, Ivor thought he was ready for anything…except tiny buttons. At first Ivor put his arms tenderly around Marian and kissed her, a long deep kiss. His eager fingers found a row of fastenings all down the back of her dress, as far as Marian's bottom. What was this?

He kissed her neck. She shivered. He turned her around and gently started to undo the top button. It was difficult, but he managed it. He kissed her neck again and murmured into her ear. The second button was no easier than the first.

Jeez! This is going to take all night!

He said softly, 'Isn't there an easier way to do this, darling?'

She turned back to face him and put her arms around him, 'I can't see how, sweetie. It did take some time to get me into this dress.'

'And very beautiful you look too. But you can't very well go to bed in it, can you?'

Ivor tried again on the third button. There was a gap now, sufficient for him to kiss her shoulders.

Marian was tired of standing patiently. 'I know,' she said, 'Why don't you cut the buttons off. I'll get some scissors.'

She searched her new pigskin beauty case for the tiny curved nail scissors she knew were there.

Among lots of giggles from Marian and grunts and kisses from Ivor they managed to enjoy the slow disrobing. But at last Ivor, his feet surrounded by tiny white buttons, did not feel like waiting any longer. He gripped the opened sections and pulled them apart. Buttons popped off, the fabric ripped from top to hem. He made short work of getting the designer dress off.

Then at last he carried his bride to the bed.

(Dancing feet – Linda Brooks)

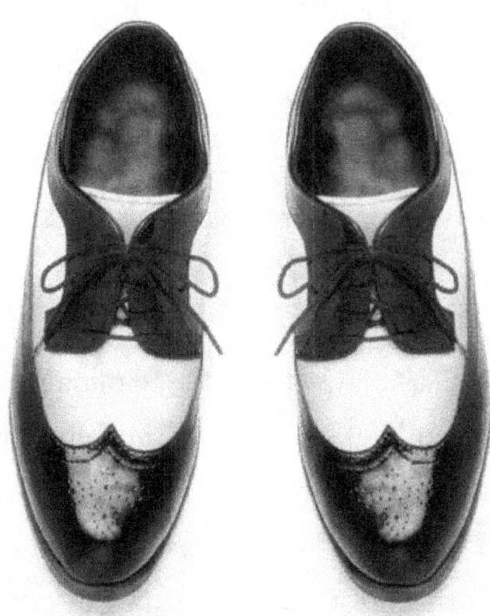

In the fifties, when I was a kid growing up in Northcote, there were two 'tribes'.

No, it was not the ones who barracked for Collingwood, and the ones who barracked for Fitzroy.

Rather it was we 'Australians' with surnames like 'McBride' and 'Doyle' and 'Moloney'; and there were the 'Italians' with surnames like 'Gaetano', 'Munzone' and 'Benedetti'. The Italians and the Australians lived side by side in tidy rows of weatherboard houses with corrugated iron roofs and picket fences. Though gradually the 'Italians' turned their weatherboard houses into brick veneer by simply covering the boards with a wall of orange brick. My mum got on marvellously with the other tribe. She liked to stop and chat.

She loved the new types of cheese you could get by calling in on them in the afternoons; she loved their parties in the backyard on weekends with music, laughter and drink. And she loved the exotic drinks they would serve up to her in little ornate glasses: the Crème de Menthe and the Marsala.

Mum never figured out any of their surnames. She would say to me: 'John, Nick down to the Italians around the corner and see if they want any of these biscuits I just made,' or 'Nick down to the Italians down the street and borrow a cup of flour'.

We coexisted, and gradually we blended. Back in Northcote at St Joseph's Primary School there were many more of 'them' than there were of 'us'. Looking at the Grade Three school photo I have in a cupboard, there are about ten of we Doyles, McBrides and Moloneys, compared to about sixty Gaetanos and Benedettis.

The two tribes travelled together along High St and Smith St on the tram on the way to school. We visited one another's houses on the way home from school. We played with one another in the yard and in the street; and we went to the footy together at the MCG on Saturday afternoons.

I knew we were different, but it wasn't until I was much older, maybe thirty or forty years down the track before I learned what the difference was. The difference, dear reader, was that they were more fashionable than us.

I am an Anglo-Saxon Australian, third generation. My great grandfather on Dad's side came over from Ireland at the end of the 19th century. Mum's grandparents came from England around the same time. I am also a public servant, and also a scientist. So, I am pretty nerdy, pretty conservative, pretty Anglo-Australian. I grew up wearing Fletcher Jones trousers, and Glo-weave shirts, with Brylcream on my hair.

As I grew older, and became an adult, and went to work I remained unfashionable. I wore a jumper to work, with a narrow tie and I carried a brown leather brief case, with a worn handle.

My second wife, on the other hand, who I married forty years later is Italian …and…she's very fashionable.

Being a good Australian man I owned two pair of shoes that I would wear to work in my office in the city. I owned a brown pair that I would wear with certain sets of clothes, and a black pair that matched all my other clothes.

One day, I was walking along the street and the sole came loose on the black pair…so, out in Collins St at lunchtime, suddenly I was walking along like Bozo the clown, with my shoe making a flop, flop, flop sound as I walked.

There are two courses of action open when your shoe reaches the end of its useful life.

The first is that you can get on the tram, travel up to Myers, and buy a replacement pair of shoes…sensible Australian shoes, made of leather, with laces, and so on.

Or… you can go home that evening and mention to your fashionable Italian wife that you need a new pair of shoes. I did the latter.

So the following weekend my fashionable Italian wife organises me so that we get in the car and drive out to Coburg to the shoe factories and outlet stores. I walk in to one of these outlet shoe places…there are shoes displayed in boxes all around the perimeter of the factory wall…I see a nice conservative looking replacement pair…lace-up, leather…the sort I've worn all my life.

I take the shoe off the box and am trying it on. Then I look up and see my wife and the factory owner…an elder, very fashionable-looking Italian gent looking at me, shaking their heads.

The next thing I know I am handed a pair of two-tone shoes…the left side of the shoe is white…the right side is black. The shoe is made of leather, with laces; but it has the lines and the style of a running shoe.

I panic.

I look around for help…there is no help…my wife and the factory owner are insistent…I try the shoes on…we buy them.

Next Monday I am in at work…walking the corridors, attending the seminar, having scientific discussions, joining my friends for morning tea…all in two-tone Italian shoes. They laugh. They snigger. At the beginning of the seminar, after presenting the highly mathematical title of the talk, the speaker breaks the ice and engages the audience by making a joke about two-tone shoes.

The following week I was due to fly up to Brisbane to attend a special Conference on the topic of Australian Storms, organised jointly by the Meteorological Societies of Australia and New Zealand. I was speaking with my boss, the famous scientist Neville Nicholls before I left:

'You're not going to wear those shoes to Brisbane?' he asked jokingly in disbelief.

I went home that night to pack for the conference. My fashionable Italian wife insisted I wear the two-tone shoes.

I was giving two presentations at the Storms Conference – One on tropical cyclones and one on what is likely to happen to major rainfall events under global warming. The first day of the conference seemed to go well. Though at the opening ice-breaker and at the morning tea breaks, there seemed to be a lot of discussion about shoes. I called my wife from the hotel that evening.

'There are about two hundred scientists up here in Brisbane', I said. 'One hundred and ninety nine of them seem to be joking about my shoes.

Being an older scientist, I get a bit of a kick out of engaging the younger scientists and the students at tea breaks and lunch sessions at these meetings. On the following day, I was talking to an attractive young female scientist, probably in her thirties as we helped ourselves to scones while we juggled our saucer and tea cup.

'I like your shoes', she said. I tried to steer the conversation to tropical cyclone dynamics.

Later that day, I went with a group for lunch in a local sandwich bar. This group also included a number of younger female scientists and PhD students. I was sitting with one of them while we ate and chatted about careers and about Brisbane. She paused mid-conversation, and said, 'By the way, I love those shoes. They really suit you.'

That afternoon, I gave the first of my two conference presentations, the one on tropical cyclones. I always feel drained after the experience of putting together a major presentation like that; so I left the conference early that day, and walked by myself back towards the hotel.

On the way, I stopped at another little sandwich bar to have a coffee and to relax.

As I was sitting there at an outside table, I heard the voice of a young waitress as she approached: 'Hey…what a great pair of shoes!'

Before I go on, I have to point out what we are dealing with here. This is John, in his fifties, scientist, nerd, has been unfashionable all his life.

I phoned my wife again from the hotel:

'I've changed my mind', I said, 'I like these shoes.'

And I flew back to Melbourne and to work the following week, and I wore those two-tone shoes every day to work in the city and to the various scientific conferences I attended around the nation. I wore them until the soles were worn down. Eventually one Sunday evening, they were finished, and I carried them out to the street and placed them in the rubbish bin out there on the nature strip.

And that is the story of the two-tone shoes.

Tower of Ivory
Touch of purple
Purple for Prince
Prince of the Church –
Keeper of the Keys

Tiny purple buttons marched down the black soutane, swelled on the massive frame, topped by the black biretta. 'Upon this rock I will build my church.' Monsignor stood often among the plaster frogs among the rocks in the church-yard surrounded by chattering school-girls.

'Bless me father for I have sinned.'

Confession over, any moment now he would pinch someone's hat elastic in retribution for venial crimes – let his hand come to rest on Annette's golden curls.

Solid he stood in his upward march to Heaven. Solid in his never once doubted belief in an unchanging God. Fifty years a priest and the parish persevered in preparations for a golden jubilee concert.

Irish song and dance paid tribute to his transplant to these foreign rocks. Gymnastics, verse speaking and choral items culminating in a tableau – the family at prayer smiled down upon by the Virgin Mary.

Monsignor was sold on the Virgin Mary. I remember he told us one Benediction sermon how he had forgotten his rosary beads and returned home to get them. The train he was on his way to catch had met with a minor derailment but he had felt that forgetting his beads had in some way been a miracle of saving. I wondered about the other passengers with no beads to forget or remember but for him that happening intensified his devotion to Mary.

For the tableaux I had been chosen to represent the Virgin Mary. My mother was Jewish and my Irish father what is known in charity as a 'lapsed Catholic'. There had been no nepotism on Sister Theophile's part. Sister Theophile taught art mainly – she was an artist in her own right – painting some fine oils and architect-designing the college chapel. She was a great teacher of geography too - really made things live and I remember her geometry lessons where you felt a sense of achievement when you solved a problem – we would even stay back after school to try and work out equal angles.

I was dark. The boys called me 'Indian'. Summers in the Cronulla surf meant my skin was really brown. We were rehearsing the tableaux when Monsignor strode into the hall, stopped midway his voice boomed toward the stage: 'The mother of God is fair, golden as the morning.' It was a statement of fact.

Sister Theophile carefully descended the stepladder and slowly advanced to the front of the stage. An actress delivering her lines her voice filled the hall: 'Christ was a Jew Monsignor, of that there can be no doubt, and I think I am correct in assuming his mother was also Jewish.'. The plaster angels trembled. The paper flowers massed around the stage seemed to wilt. Dark complexioned, long black hair, I stood trembling and wilting at the top of the choir steps. Monsignor did not answer, he turned and left.

Serenely Sister Theophile returned to the tableaux. Admiration and awe welled around her. It was no mean feat for anyone, least of all a nun, to cross the Monsignor. She rearranged the heavy blue drapes that hung around me.

'I want them to look solid as though sculptured,' she said, 'to give a timeless quality.' I could see her hands tremble slightly. The conviction I would be struck dead for daring to play the mother of God haunted me and combined with real stage fright was highlighted by Monsignor's outburst. He knew my spiritual state.

'Bless me father for I have sinned.' The commandments scrupulously examined a spotlight to search out the most intimate flaw. I even wrote out lists of sins. 'To do the right thing for the wrong reason', that always troubled me. Looking back I guess I could be described at best as 'over conscientious'. The night of the concert came. The lights dimmed for the finale. The curtains opened.

In one corner of the stage a family knelt in prayer. Behind stretched sheet-draped choir steps – midway up - stood two angels, their wings slightly off centre despite all Sister Theophile's efforts, their arms offering long streamers of paper roses. I stood, looking like an almost sacrificial figure, arms stretched earthwards, eyes downcast, trying for an enigmatic smile over a 'slight touch of powder'. I waited for the roof to open and the wrath of Heaven to descend.

'Tower of Ivory...House of Gold'

Virgin of Virgins (at least at 14 that was in my favour). The litany of praise filled the hall. Somewhere out there sat my proud parents and brothers, and friends who had been dragooned into coming. Somewhere out there, too, sat the Monsignor affronted by my lack of Nordic beauty and the vision no doubt of my shrivelled soul. I was exposed. Transparent. Each weekly confession had stripped my soul layer by layer like the skins of an onion. Behind me one of the senior girls tottered on a ladder, a torch held behind my head so as to create a halo effect. I felt hatred, real or imagined. My teenage children would call it 'vibes' now: hatred for the dark complexion, the subtle mystery of my mother's race, the age old hatred of one race for another – of Gentile for Jew.

I swayed at the apex of the triangle but the roof of the parish hall held firm. The curtains swished to a close. My final nightmare though was still to come.

I caught the train to the city. There was no way I could face confession at Cronulla. I went to Saint Patrick's in the heart of Sydney. There I was anonymous. And I still love the quiet beauty of that church.

'Bless me father for I have sinned – I have sinned against the fifth commandment.'

'Thou shalt not kill, my child?'

'Yes Father. I have hated someone Father – worse still I have hated Christ's representative.'

'I have hated a priest, Father…'

The Department of Human Services provides a range of 'services' to people with disabilities and their families. Knowing your entitlements is often hard to establish. Bureaucrats give you part of the overall picture. As parents we spent hours on the phone, standing in queues and attending meetings. After Adam finished at school at the age of 21 we discovered his name was no longer on the Disability Services Register. That was strange, as he was on it when he was younger. In 1972, at two months of age, he was diagnosed with a severe disability. He spent several years as a young child in an early intervention program at the Children's Hospital. He attended Day Training Centres for ten years, until he was thirteen. Adam would never have had access to any of these facilities without being registered with The Department of Human Services. The Day Training Centres were overseen by the Health Department, and one would have hoped they were on speaking terms with Human Services.

From 13 years to 21 years of age Adam attended his local school with the support of an integration program. It seemed that because Adam attended a regular school, he had moved out of the Government's bureaucratic support systems and fallen off the Disability Services Register 'tree.' Several of his friends who had kept the status quo by remaining at the Centres had stayed on the Register and were now living in group-homes.

We knew we were doing the right thing by supporting and fighting for Adams right to attend his local school. The Education Department, despite its faults had been able to work with us while he was enrolled in his school. Many professionals involved in education have the ability to look laterally and problem solve. In most cases they are able to work with others in developing solutions for complex situations. On the other hand the Department of Human Services have a totally different view of the world and are usually unable to problem solve effectively. Whether it is lack of funding, stress, attitude or other factors, Education and Human Services Departments are diametrically opposed in how they think and operate. It took several more years before Adam was able to climb back up the bureaucratic tree and regain his place back on the register.

Place

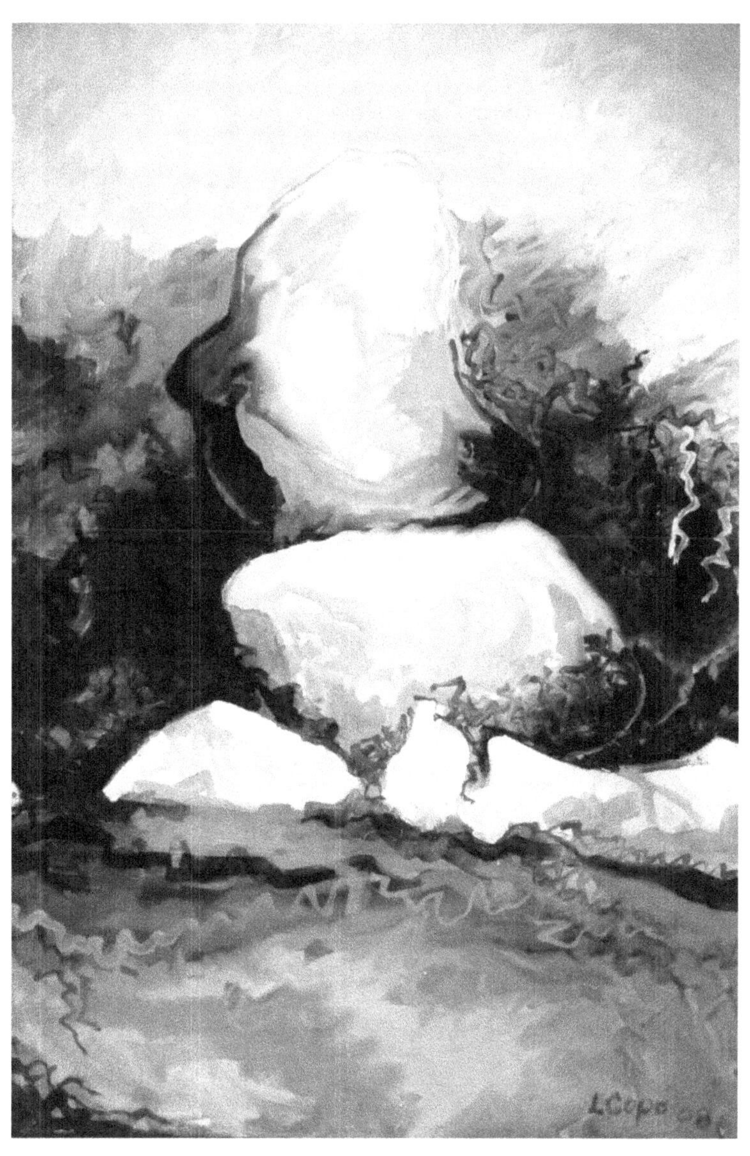

Home - Magdalena Ball

Here
in blue green mountain tops
alone
with magpies, Rosella flash, heartbreaking currawong gargle
noise
grown familiar beneath the skin
like the traffic jam horns and overheard arguments
of childhood
background noise you know
below the surface of consciousness

it's that time of the year
pink stamens on blue gums
Eucalyptus globulus
clears the sinus

the earth beneath my fingers
crumbles into something essentially
Antipodean
home
and not home
dislocation mingling with familiarity
that dream you can't shake
Sunday roast
dysfunctional family welcome
you can't join

every now and then
when birds stop singing
long enough

that other voice – the hungry, pouting banshee

grabs you, surprise

pushing silent dialogue

drawing a long thread of lost and found

tangling here and there

into one murky space

that reconstitutes itself

into the astringent, vegetative

present.

Olivia stepped off the Gang Plank onto new soil and a new life. New for her anyway. As she was to learn, the soil was as ancient as it could possibly be. The five weeks since she had left that other ancient world, a world of picture-book English cottages, pebbly beaches, and cold, snowy winters, had been lonely. More lonely than any time she could remember.

Now, she realised the truth. Her life was not really meant to be lived as a single person. Always there had been someone to share thoughts, dreams; even activities. But living here would be a challenge. There would be new friends, of both sexes. At 'home', besides her parents and her sister, she had never been short of someone to talk to. She expected no problem in that area.

She had asked someone on the ship how to get to the city of Sydney. He had told her which bus to catch, where to stand for the bus stop and how often they ran. So it would not be a problem on this first day of November to go sight-seeing. She had until 5pm when she was due back on the ship. The bus came at the time it was expected and she asked to be set down at Sydney. The conductor was puzzled.

'This is Sydney, Miss.'

'Yes. I want to go to the...the...city.'

'Wynyard. That OK?'

'Er, yes. Yes, that will do. Will you tell me when we are there?'

'Yes, Miss.'

Sitting on the bus she felt that all eyes were on her, but that couldn't be so. It was just that everything was so new and unexpected. Certainly nothing looked in the least like London. She had been used to walking around that great Metropolis, usually with her friend, Elsie. They had shared lots of laughs, dreams, and ambitions as well as being partners in their stage act. But when Elsie said she didn't want to continue with their act because it had meant spending most of the time in the North Country, Olivia had decided to migrate to Australia.

Olivia had to admit that the North Country, while providing most of their work, was not the most appealing part of the British Isles, and what was worse the winters were something she had dreaded every year as they came around. All that slushy snow and ice!

It was a New Zealand guy who had suggested Australia to her. He said he wouldn't recommend New Zealand. He had come to England was to pursue his career in photography. There were so few opportunities in his home country.

This bus seems to be going on forever! The conductor is upstairs. He's forgotten me.

She got off the bus. Standing on the pavement she looked around her. The streets appeared to be a bit old fashioned. That surprised her, this is a modern city, surely! She turned to the left and started walking downhill. After a while she saw a sort of arcade. Interesting. She turned into it. A few quaint shops leading shortly into another street. Here there were houses. A row of them, all the same. And all looking grey. Stone, of course. With small windows and neat doors fronting on to the street. But nobody about.

She kept walking. When she got to the end of the street, she crossed over and started back. It would not do to get lost in this strange place, there was no-one to ask the way. Perhaps everybody was at home for lunch. Back on the main street she saw a cafe. She entered and sat down. On the menu were things she didn't recognise, but she did know about hamburgers and milk shakes. She ordered those. She wished she hadn't worn her smart English wool suit. It was a natural choice to go to the city in smart clothes. That was what she was used to. But she noticed that everybody was wearing summer frocks, and they appeared to be even lighter than the few she had brought. What was it the man at Immigration who'd asked? 'Are you sure you want to go to Queensland?'

'Doesn't the tropic of Capricorn go through there?' Olivia had replied.

'Yes. That's right.'

'Then that is where I want to go,' she'd said, firmly.

He'd nodded, 'If that's what you want. No less than three cotton frocks a day there.'

She was beginning to wonder about her clothing choices. It is warm. Seems almost warmer than when they were stranded on a sand bank in the Suez Canal, with the air conditioning out of order. One of the hazards of a ship's maiden voyage. She took her jacket off and put it on the seat beside her. Seconds later a woman hovered near. 'Is this seat taken?'

'No. No.' Olivia put the jacket across her knee.

The woman ordered and turned to Olivia. 'It's a bit warm today.'

Olivia smiled at her. 'Yes, it is rather.' They were soon chatting like old friends and Olivia wondered if all the Australian people would be like this. If this was so, she would soon feel at home among them. Everything will be fine. She sat as long as she could, but the cafe was beginning to fill so she said goodbye to her new friend, paid the bill and left. She didn't feel much like spending time in this heat with the wrong clothes on so she waited for a bus. When it came she asked to be set down at the wharf for the 'Iberia'.

'No problem luv.' the conductor said. It was the same man as before. He stood close. 'What did yer think of the Rocks?'

'Oh. Interesting.' So that was where she'd been – not the city at all. She made a mental note to learn more about the Rocks. It would give her something to put in her letters home.

Back on the ship she went quickly to the shared cabin. It was empty. Most of the others had disembarked at Melbourne. A few had already gone to Sydney this morning. She wondered how they were getting on now. There was only one other girl going to Brisbane and she'd not been very talkative anyway. Olivia quickly shrugged off the Autumn-weight suit and put on some shorts. Then she spent some time sorting out clothes, removing some from the trunk to replace those in the suitcase. Would she ever need that suit again?

She would spend some time writing home. She could also send a letter to Elsie. Remember to ask after Tom, the boy friend who'd somehow got in the way of their decisions. Certainly she knew Elsie expected a proposal from Tom soon. She sealed the letter and put it with the one to her parents. The helpful Immigration officials would post them for her.

Tomorrow there would be sorting with the authorities. Those travelling to Queensland faced a train trip. The next surprises would be the length of that train journey. The excitement of seeing the first kangaroos, the differences, the boredom of the scenery, and the lack of train stations.

No doubt about it. Everything is new. The future will be a different sort of challenge.

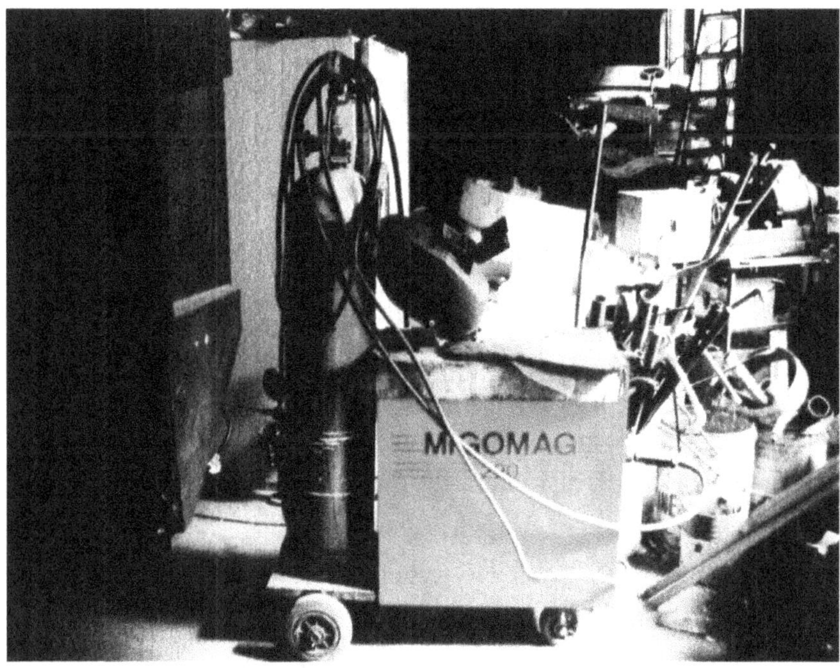

Along the journey of my unconventional childhood, I was introduced to the great Australian shed. As Australians, we are excessively fond of our sheds. My theory regarding this lies in our convict heritage. After all, we arrived in this harsh land, with nothing but the chains on our feet. The ships that brought us here carried more guns and soldiers than tools. Ingenuity was mandatory. If the aristocracy had arrived without the convict element they would soon have died; manual labour was of more value in this new land than following correct morning-tea rituals. Of course, it's only a theory.

At first, when very young, I thought the shed was where Dad hid from Mum. Later on, I discovered that although there may have been some truth to this assumption, there was so much more to Dad's shed. It was chock full of useful tools that Dad used to make marvellous things. I was constantly fascinated and often joined him there, and the fact that this was a place of gentle harmony added to the appeal.

Mum would get up a full head of steam to tackle the housework, taking on the mantle of martyred slavery. Mops, buckets and vacuum cleaners would appear. Dad would stand near the back door and clear his throat.

'I'm just ducking out to the shed, Else,' he'd say. I would stand next to him.

'I'm duckin' too,' I would add, holding my breath and crossing my fingers. Escape was so near but so far. Because we were both deemed hopeless at assisting Mum in the housework that began at dawn and ended at midnight, she'd let us go with a weary sigh. Mum seemed afraid of the shed, with its smells of metal, the noise and sparks of the welding machine and the oil and grime. I remember her storming in there only once and promptly putting her foot in the sump oil Dad was recycling. She gave us a short speech on 'the filth of the pair of you' and the dangers of dirt in general, but as she was discomforted by an oily foot, she very soon left us to our mess.

I wondered on this occasion, as I had on many others, if these kinds of incidents were not quite as accidental as they appeared, but strategies of my father to discourage her from entering his domain. He wouldn't have been the only male in history to do so. Dad gave no sign of this, but at times he could be inscrutable. He was orderly and precise, enjoying his world of tools and tinkering immensely, whistling as he worked. On the shed wall was a board with hooks and holes and the outline of whatever belonged there. In my mind the shed was a tidy place although every bench was cluttered with projects in various stages of completion, unlike inside where not a crumb was allowed to linger on floor or table. The shed was a different kind of *tidy* than inside the house. His tools were always in their proper place in his own system. Engine parts, gas bottles and cables were allowed on the floor, but he never misplaced anything.

Dad made wrought iron gates and trims. All our car repairs were undertaken by him, and later by my brother. There were tyres he was re-treading, deepening the groove with a hot electric thing that looked like a soldering iron. I can't even remember what it was called because I learned very little about the things he did, and much about the patient focus with which he approached each task. He kept his tools clean with a kerosene soaked rag. He had an old empty peach tin with an inch of kerosene and a rag in it. This was a job I often requested, just to be near him. I sat quietly on the floor making sure all the grime was wiped off his tools or an engine part. If Mum had bothered to look, she would have been shocked to see me curled up contentedly on the rough cement floor, quietly and diligently polishing Dad's tools. I, who seemed allergic to cleaning anything, and showed all the signs consistent with domestic failure. I, who never sat still.

Just under the ceiling of the shed Dad had positioned wire meshing the length and breadth of the shed. He hung lights from this in various positions to illuminate whatever part of the car engine he was currently fixing. Although this marvellous system served his lighting purposes effectively, he allowed me to think I was indispensable by holding the torch for him. I would do this for hours, shining the beam exactly where he needed it, while he talked about gearboxes and how to care for them so the gears wouldn't grind and shear off. He explained pistons, talked about carburettors and how the clutch worked.

Never quite grasping his skills or passion for those things—I did learn about life and unconditional love within these lessons about machinery and tools. I learned that if you wanted something to last you had to take care of it. Among the vices, electric saws, spanners, nuts and bolts, there were always collections of paint cans and airbrushes. Dad made signs for the church notice board and pungent paint fumes filled the shed, along with the smells of the welder. And there were several soldering irons and grinders that filled the air with the smell of metal shavings and hot molten solder.

It was a wonder we weren't a bit high on the cacophony of smells. We were certainly happy out there. years later, after his death, I visited Sovereign Hill, the tourist attraction in Victoria. I stood transfixed with unexpected tears when I walked into 'Ye Olde Blacksmith's'.

It smelled like home.

(Toepfer's shed – photograph by Ray Dobson)

Hunter Street, Newcastle, NSW - Louise Berry

wide pavement accommodates
skinny skateboarders
showing off for office workers
bathed in evening light
strolling to the station

occasionally a man
clutching a brown papered bottle
in a hand divorced from cleanliness
shuffles along the bricks
telling the world of his delusions

plump women cut off from the world
ears stuffed with noise
jaws masticating
waddle slowly towards shops
and a take-away meal

shirt rumpled businessmen
spiky-haired
rush to the bottle shop
return clutching paper covered parcels
in anticipation of relaxation

the roar of re-worked engines
shatters the dying light
reawakening energy
dissipated by service
to the altar of survival

the street renews
as the light fades
those seeking amusement
stroll arm in arm

talk in muted voices
 as the clock strikes midnight
only night owls
sit under the starry sky
or sleep in doorways
enjoying the stillness

morning light
warms shopkeepers
pulling up shutters

glancing around
trying to assess
the quality of the day

aware profits
rely on weather
for health

in midday heat
bargain hunters
pick over seller's wares

wander from stall to stall
exclaim aloud
at each new discovery

excited children
lick on ice-creams
run underfoot

late afternoon
there's a lull
as the street waits
for its life
to start again

We sat in silence and gloomily peered through the misty windows of our family car at the main street of Adelong. It had taken us several long hours to make the arduous 284 mile trip along the Hume Highway from Sydney. We were tired, not to mention just a little irritable, and we were finding it very difficult to share in Dad's excitement about our new hometown.

The cold winter rain pelted down on the sedan roof and windows and added to the bleak mood that had begun to permeate the car interior.

'Is this *it*?' my sister asked in a grim voice - just *slightly* tinged with hope that Dad might say something like, 'No! Of course not! We're just stopping here for a break…'

Sadly, my father's response was one that we were all dreading.

'Yes, this is it!'

I couldn't believe it.

When Dad and Mum had first announced to us four kids that Dad had bought his own accountancy business 'in the country' and that we would be leaving Sydney, I wasn't sure what to think about it. It was 1964 and I was 12 years old. The thought of leaving my home, Grandparents, my church and school friends … all that was familiar to me, was a little daunting.

Even so, there was alongside the fear of the unknown, a rather 'grown-up' sense of adventure that presented itself. Dad had softened the blow about leaving Sydney by explaining that living 'in the country' would be like living at Auntie Doll and Uncle Jack's place. Aunty Doll and Uncle Jack lived on a dairy farm on the NSW South Coast, and we kids had wonderful memories of visits filled with fun and laughter trying to milk the cows at the dairy, being chased by cranky bulls in the paddock, hiding in the hay sheds, tractor rides, and great country cooking…mmm, what kid *wouldn't* want to live in the country! Dad also pointed out that we would be able to own bikes in the country – because it was a lot safer to ride them there than in the city. *Yes!* I'd always wanted a 2-wheeler bike!

A couple of weeks later Mum and Dad took us 'in to town' to David Jones to buy some new clothes for our future new life in the country. Because we were going to live in the Snowy Mountains, we needed to stock up on winter woollies. I chose a tan and black hounds-tooth pinafore and coat, some tartan tights and 'sensible' shoes. These shopping outings in the centre of Sydney were rare for us as a family, so this added to the importance of the new direction our lives were about to take.

But on this *first* day of our 'new life in the country', this first miserably grey and wet day parked in the main street of Adelong, all thoughts of adventure seem to evaporate. Looking out through the relentless pounding of raindrops at the old wooden buildings, together with ancient gnarled and naked trees (spattered with starling droppings) that lined the main street, it was hard to feel optimistic about our new life!

Dad had parked the car outside an old building that looked as though it was about to fall over. The word *Accountant* was painted across the glass front door and Dad told us this was his 'new' office.

Silence.

We all got out and looked over the new office. Mmmm……

After we got back into the car, we each suddenly found our voices and began passionately expressing our change of heart about moving to the country! Poor Dad – looking back now he must have been a bit discouraged himself – but there was no way he was letting on to us. We drove another 12 miles to Tumut where we stayed the night in a motel. Tumut was a much bigger, more 'civilised' town. I'm not sure how it happened, but somewhere in the night a decision was reached that the family would live in Tumut, not Adelong, and that Dad would drive the 12 miles to work each day (thanks Mum!).

And so it was.

For the next 13 years my family lived a country life in Tumut and my Dad drove the 12 miles to Adelong each day, six days a week, to The Office. I lived with them until I left school and moved to Teachers' College in Wagga Wagga, a large city with a population of 60,000 or so, around 65 miles away from home.

In the early days of my country life there were some adjustments to be made.

Entering my teen years in the country did have some definite drawbacks. The all-important fashion stakes for one. The Tumut Co-Op had little to offer a contemporary teen, but fortunately for my sister and I our family made regular trips back to Sydney to visit our grandparents, and this occasionally meant purchasing some new clothes as well. My country friends would be green with envy on my return when I announced that I had bought whatever I was wearing in *Sydney*!

This was also my first experience in attending a co-ed school. *And* having a male teacher!

It was all a little odd at first, but once I fell in love with Christopher Simpson, everything seemed to fall into place.

I admit to feeling a certain amount of pride at having come from the *Big City* and this was reinforced by the subtle admiration of my new-found friends. At first I deliberately resisted the

Country Bumpkin ways of my new world, although secretly enjoying the warmth and openness of country folk. There was a freedom and easiness of life there that even as an 12 year old I was conscious of and appreciated.

Dad bought a lovely block of land in Tumut, high on a hill overlooking the town and eventually built a very contemporary and unusual home for us there. Mum's brother was an architect and so had volunteered to design it. The house was the talk of the town for many years.

Dad made friends with the Adelong community – most of whom had become his clients. Many of these clients were 'on the land' - graziers and farmers – and occasionally we would visit them on their properties. I remember loving the rides on tractors, or in the back of the jeeps, as the farmer would proudly (and bumpily) show us around his property. After the tour we'd arrive back at the farmhouse and get stuck into the lavish afternoon tea set out on the table. Huge scones with jam and cream, pikelets, sponge cakes and the like laid out of the best family china plates. Dad has always been interested in yarns about the past and he would encourage these men to share their stories of life on the land. I loved listening in. Many times Dad would come home from The Office with a 'beast' – a sheep or calf – that a farmer had slaughtered and cut up, to give to Dad in lieu of paying for tax work. The beast filled our freezer and kept us in meat for months. These country people were so generous and friendly.

The simplicity of country life fostered a community spirit that isn't easily found in the city. Family lives continually interacted in a variety of ways. For example, my friend Judy's parents owned the Fruit Shop, Libby's parents owned the local Jewellers store, Elizabeth's parents owned the local cinema (once, on Elizabeth's 16th birthday, her Dad let us all into the cinema to watch a private viewing of the latest James Bond movie!), and our (unpaid) church minister owned the local Pharmacy.

Because Dad was friends with the police officer in Adelong, it made it easy for me to get my driver's licence through him, rather than to go through one of the Driving Schools. When we were building our house, Dad's contacts in the local building trade helped with cost price articles. AND because he knew the owner of Adelong Produce Store, we had *free* (used) plastic fertiliser bags to use in lieu of toboggans when we went to Kiandra's snowfields on weekends! It didn't take me too long to accept the Country Bumpkin way of life.

Since those childhood days I have lived in various places – some towns, some cities. I have come to truly love and value the variety of people and communities that comprise this wonderful nation of ours.

Seasons of the Trees - Jo Tregellis

five trees

line the road

outside my home

telling the seasons

to my soul.

bare branches

scrape the sky

long before I have time

to note the vanity

of showy leaves.

so soon

the green tinge

of jealous leaves

springs out

to remind me

that I envy their spontaneity.

full summer glory –

in the canopies' spread

of comforting shade

I rest, and

can't help but wonder.

Cracker Night at Wombarra Heights - Jo Hanrahan

It would soon be Cracker Night up in the bush at Wombarra Heights. For weeks, the neighbours had been collecting firewood and dumping it on Harrison's Green in readiness. Everyone would be there – Who could miss the best night of the year? Cracker Night. The pile of wood was getting bigger every day. Soon it would be as big as Harrison's house.

Excitement was in the air. This year it was to be more spectacular than ever before. Fathers were stocking up on crackers for the fireworks, and mothers were making sure the potato box was full of spuds. Anyone knows you can't have a Cracker Night without spuds. As the day drew near, the woodpile for the bonfire grew even higher.

As twilight gathered, people began to arrive. Stinky Aston was the first to arrive; followed y 'Bruiser' Lenham and 'Dummy' Harris – all carrying bundles of kindling. Dummy couldn't speak or hear, but that didn't bother him – he enjoyed himself just the same. And everyone liked him. Boxes of crackers were dumped on his mother's veranda by Georgy Harrison and a few of his mates. Kids came from everywhere. The bush kids wouldn't miss Cracker Night for quids. They had talked of nothing else for weeks. Mickey Myerscoff, from across the gully came early. Tommy and Teddy Potts, and Jackie Harris from over near the sawmill came together. Jackie's mate, young Phil Owen, tramped up the road. Stocky young Albert Anilzark strolled nonchalantly down the bush track nearby. Lanky 'Squeaker' Dodds, little 'Bluey' DeCluet and smart Darby Ranger converged from opposite sides of The Green.

'Tiddy' and 'Tubby' Parkinson, the terrible twins, slunk over after dark to ogle the girls. Sexy Violie Ashton peered around at the boys as she glided onto The Green in her tight, slinky dress. 'Pommy' Gray, with his sisters Velie and Josie, came quietly to the sidelines. 'Eggy' Vigal had come up along the main road to meet with his girlfriend, Blondie Hindmarsh, who lived across the paddock. He's been sweet on her for ages. She arrived shortly afterwards with a big bag of spuds – he blonde hair in a perfect pageboy, sleek as ever.

Darkness fell. Amid cheers and shouting the fire was lit. Flames shot heavenward – raging higher and higher. Smoke billowed ominously. Mrs Harrison, whose house fronted The Green, began to look worried. Whoosh went the rockets. Zing went the Catherine Wheels. And everywhere could be heard the Pop! Pop! of the Tom Thumbs. All the while the kids of the bush squealed in delight. Gradually, as the chill settled in over The Green, the fire started to die down. There wasn't much wood left to feed it. Eventually all the fireworks were gone, the bungers collected and refired as fizzers. The lost ones would be found in the morning. The firewood had burned down. Embers glowed. This was the next highlight of the evening. Where were the spuds? The bushes parted as the small children crept back with bags and boxes of spuds raided from their mother's pantries.

Then, the real fun began. Stomachs rumbled as spuds turned black among the embers. Garden forks and rakes – anything that wouldn't burn – were called into service to drag those little black beauties from the almost spent ash of the fire. The delicious smell of potato flesh rose as crusty skins were broken to reveal their snowy white insides. The feast lasted into the wee hours of the morning. Sated and relaxed, everyone agreed that this years' Cracker Night was the best yet. The cleanup could wait until tomorrow.

Whale Song - Jennifer Goard

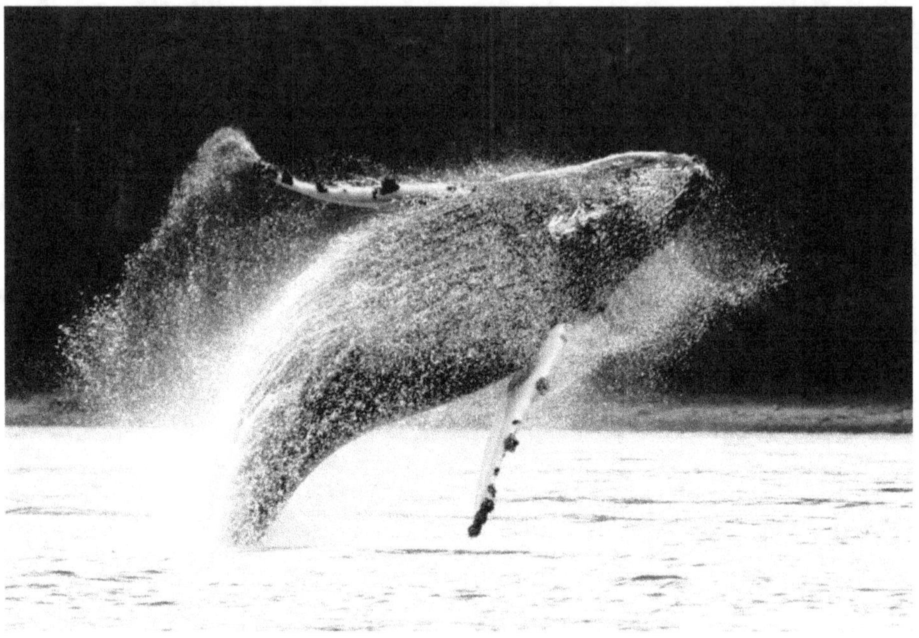

Blue! The deepest, darkest blue departs from the abyss of the time traveller. A noise! A far away noise piercing the silence of the all encompassing blue. I roll my vision up towards the filtered streams of light, stretching down from the surface into the blue depths below me. Moving with purposeful motion towards the light, I need to reach the source of life and replenish my lungs.

Near now, the dark blue has turned to aqua, then a beautiful shimmering turquoise surrounds my body, caressing. I become languid in the change of temperature filtering around me as I ascend towards the surface. Up, up and suddenly, I'm there, my head breaking through the silken barrier that separates two very different worlds.

My blow hole follows my face. With my last breath I push water out in a spray. It remains in the sky above creating mist that catches the rays of the sun. Colourful halos swirl through the vapour. I breathe in the sweet air, tasting the exotic odours that waft on the gentle sea breezes that have travelled across the water from lands far beyond.

It amazes me that after so many millenniums our families still have to leave the safety of the deep to breathe oxygen from above. The air also delights my skin. I leap out of the water, flipping weightlessly, for no reason, just because I am here—alive. Crashing down onto the surface creates spume and foam. I see other fountains of water surging upward. My family! My kin: all living and breathing the air with the joy of being on the surface once more. With lungs full of the life force we prepare to dive again, just a minor detour to the journey along 'The Great Route'. I plunge my head into the warm water. With a heave I propel the rest of my body down again, the last flicking of my tail is the only reminder of my presence above.

Down, down and away I drift, away from the aqua and shimmering turquoise, away from the warmth. Past the streaming filtered light from above and into the deep, deep blue. In The Deep Blue our Whale Song lilts, rising and falling—reaching out to Family.

Now, the travelling song is passing between us. It is our constant companion on our way south. Our song is as old as the ocean itself; it is how we find each other in the depths. The song collects our thoughts, sending them forth into the Deep Blue so we can share the family mind. As I flow along with the deep strong current, I join the singing to share with the others what I experienced when I surfaced. My song echoes through the vastness and the rhythm entwines with the family song and I am comforted. I am not alone.

Not so long ago our families were killed as they travelled the ancient routes. They were dragged out of the ocean; we tasted their filtered blood through the water. Our songs into the void brought no response. It was the loneliest feeling in all of the Deep Blue. We were lost.

Something changed over time and our families survived. We grew in numbers and our songs filled the oceans once more. The song changes its tone and rhythm—a sign we are almost at our destination. The temperature has gradually dropped, bringing with it a change in the colour of the sea. Whiteness abounds and emerald cold brings an abundance of food.

The family of travellers ascend once more—as one. I glide ever upwards, breaking the icy surface. Once again I force the water out in a shower of celebration and breathe the sweet cold air of the south. Our song gives thanks to the great universal source that provides the family safety. Our minds contemplate the getting of wisdom, food and creating new life.

Until we move north again.

Snake - Rina Robinson

While working in the garden bed
one morning, with a rake
I thought I saw a lizard,
but no, it was a snake.

Only a very tiny one,
but enough to turn me sour.
Enough to make me cry out loud,
and spoil my happy hour

My neighbour heard me yell.
He said 'What is the matter?'
I answered, 'I think I've got a snake!'
It wasn't idle chatter.

He said, 'But it's only a baby one.'
I said, 'There may be more!
Perhaps there is a mother snake
And baby snakes galore!'

My neighbour chopped the thing in half
and made a charming bow.
He smiled, 'You'd best get used to them,
you're in Australia now.'

Long after that my garden grew -
I'd planted lots of seeds.
But in that place where the snake had been
there's only tangled weeds.

Before the earthquake of 1989, Newcastle NSW was known as a 'large industrial town.' After the earthquake of 1989 Newcastle NSW was known as 'that large industrial town that had an earthquake'. In the twenty years since the earthquake, she has since become less of an industrial town and a little bit closer to a modern, bohemian city whose population used to remember the natural disaster every year, but now only does so every five or ten years.

What I hated was I was not in my home town when the earthquake hit. I was in Coffs Harbour on holiday with my younger brother, Philip; a mate, Tony; and my brother's mate, Darren. This is how it all went down. At the then mature age of 23, I was 'absent without leave' when my city had its biggest event since the flaming car Star Hotel riots of 1979 that shortly after was immortalised by Aussie rockers Cold Chisel.

We'd crept into a Coffs Harbour caravan park around mid-afternoon on December 27th 1989, tired after Christmas and Boxing Day celebrations, and a little jetlagged by the trip from Newcastle—a jetlagged feeling even though we travelled there by car, if that makes any sense.

We constructed a slipshod tent and I crashed in there immediately despite the hot weather. To my confusion, I awoke an hour later in the orange light to the sound of giggling and the sight of a little green crab that was inching itself towards me, pincers ready—I believed—to sever my little toes. The giggling was not the crab, as you might have gathered, but the other guys outside who did this sort of thing for a lark all the time, as we all did.

That night we walked from the caravan park in our going to town clothes, my then long hair split-enzy because I used Sunlight Soap instead of shampoo in the caravan shower block. Anyway, at a club we drank expensive watered down scotches and Cokes, watched music videos on a big screen and then hours later walked back to the caravan park with that 'paid too much to not to get anywhere' feeling.

Next morning on December 28th we woke up around 9am, dressed casually and shortly after went by car into town to grab breakfast. On the way back, Darren, who was driving, decided to bunny hop his car around another caravan park. Inevitably the clutch cable snapped. We then pushed the car in the heat to the local Mitsubishi parts place, the rest of us hoping that this example of buffoonery would cost Darren a motza. It didn't. He wasn't called Lucky the Cat for nothing. The clutch cable for his model of Sigma, a GE (1978), was only $20 or something. The models after the GE had cables that started at over $100.

So, being someone who worked in the car game I knew that even though Darren would be paying next to nothing for his cable, they wouldn't have one for at least a week—it might even have to come from Japan—and then he'd have to book in to get it done. Well, they had one and said they could fix it within the hour for next to nothing. Lucky the Cat strikes again.

After the car was roadworthy once more, we cruised to get lunch in the middle of Coffs. Strange things then started to happen. I went to an autoteller and was told via an onscreen message that the bank I was trying to get money from, The Newcastle Permanent, was down. Then we got back into the car and just drove around. Someone put the car radio on. There was some music and we chatted generally about nothing in particular just as the DJ said: 'And we'll give you more info on the Newcastle earthquake as it comes to hand...' Someone in the car told the others to shut up, and we waited an eternity for the DJ to get back to us. We assumed the whole thing was a joke as he played Martika's then popular cover of Carole King's 'I Feel the Earth Move'.

We all decided we had to be back in Newcastle, so we went back to the caravan park to pack. Tony and I hung around waiting for Philip and Darren and we met an old man who told us the best place to go for a bite was the RSL where we could get a baked dinner and 'exotic things like peas and carrots and potatoes'. We knew all about peas, carrots and potatoes but let him talk as he seemed to delight in telling us the marvels of baked dinners.

So, we travelled in two cars, Darren driving his car with Philip as shotgun, and Tony driving his brown metallic V8 HZ Kingswood with me in the passenger seat, both vehicles trying to get to Newcastle as quickly as possible but Tony winning due to sheer horsepower.

Tony and I eventually arrived back in Newcastle after lunch, eager to go cruise Main and see what the damage was, from Hamilton where awnings had collapsed on cars and the Newcastle Worker's Club where poker machine playing pensioners had shuffled through dust and spilled coins to try and escape the rumble of the floor.

Trouble was every stickybeak Novocastrian and rubbernecker from outside Newcastle was determined to get into Newcastle as well. The roads all the way back were packed. We sat in the car outside Wickham Gates for an eternity. We had to have a story ready as security was only allowing certain people through, turning most away who u-turned it back to where they came from. We cooked up a half-baked story that I had a brother in Merewether and was concerned for his welfare. I gave the story to the security guy and he asked where my brother lived. We hadn't thought that far ahead, and he gave us the 'good try' look and urged us to turn around, which we did. Traffic was thick going back to the suburbs, but eventually I arrived home to New Lambton while Tony left to see his family in Kotara.

My brother arrived soon after, and we relayed our stories to our parents and my younger sister who had escaped from Newcastle an hour or so before from her workplace, Spotlight, a retailer of manchester, fabric etc. My parents were worried after hearing apocalyptic stories on the radio of Newcastle totally collapsing and greeted her with relief.

When the quake happened, everyone in my street apparently went outside, not having ever been prepared for such a natural disaster. It didn't hit anywhere near as badly as in the city but still it had been a shock. When I heard this I wished I had been there, too.

News stories of the after-effects were ever-present on the media and on the streets. Novocastrians loved talking about the tragedy. Unfortunately, several people lost their lives and we watched stories on TV of relatives of the deceased reliving their stories of woe.

In the following week, the Newcastle CBD and Hamilton were turned into ghost towns, with only those who owned buildings that were deemed safe or tradesmen allowed to enter the zones. Tony was a plumber at the time and was called in to do work, so he kept the rest of us updated on the situation in town.

Being an avid amateur photographer, the following week I travelled over in my car to Tighes Hill, a suburb next to Hamilton, which had had its own shakeup. That year I had been going part-time to tech (TAFE) and I was keen to see if it had sustained any damage. It had, and I used my zoom lens SLR to photograph fallen walls, and red & white taped off areas. I also talked to some teachers who were not allowed into their workplace until they were given the okay, which was at least a week away.

A week after that, buildings started to get demolished. In Tighes Hill I stood with 50 or so curious onlookers, a lot with cameras, while a pub was knocked down. In New Lambton similar crowds gathered as the facade of the pharmacy in Orchard town Road was toppled over. The old George Hotel in town, where my Nan had worked in the '70s, was apparently too unstable and had to be knocked down, yet when they tried she held on, refusing to go, and those of us who used to go there as underage drinkers with fake photocopied boat licenses were very proud of her steadfastedness that day.

Scenes like this were repeated all over the city and suburbs. The excitement then died down and thousands of people whose homes had been damaged by the earthquake struggled to get their abodes habitable again. Some of them would wait years.

A few years later I was at university. One afternoon I was at home talking on the phone to my friend Michelle. The sliding door to my room was closed, then someone rattled it to say, I assumed, that dinner was ready or that someone was at the door to see me.

'Yeah, hang on,' I yelled out.

Michelle said: 'What in the f*** was that?'

'What was what?' I replied.

'I think that was a tremor,' she said.

'Cool,' I said, I wasn't here for the last one (in 1989).'

'Well I was,' she said. 'I'm getting outa here!'

'No, just stand under the doorframe,' I said and did just that (I had read that somewhere).

Well, she uttered something unprintable and rushed outside her flat and into the street.

It's interesting to note that at the time of the turmoil in Newcastle, where we were in Coffs Harbour was very quiet, peaceful. Tony and I had been sitting on grass in the caravan park playing chess, while in our home town of Newcastle, people ran for their lives. I can't remember who won that chess game but that doesn't matter, does it? While we were playing a peaceful game that represented war, while a peaceful city was in the midst of its own war, against nature.

Years after the earthquake, when Novocastrians told their tales, I had always felt left out, but I was soon warmed by the curiosity of others who wanted to know about my time in Coffs at the time of the quake, the very story you are reading now. It was still an earthquake story, I realised, and as relevant as any other earthquake story.

One angry blue tongue lizard - Roslyn Jewel

Well, it was like this … My fellow worker Jim and I decided to take a walk at lunchtime, just to get out of the office and into the sun for a bit. We asked another of our work colleagues, Pamela if she'd like to come with us. She was pleased to join us. She'd had a pretty bad week.

Pam is an immigrant from England and not used to our native wildlife (or in fact any wildlife by the sounds of it). A few days before, she had come into work with a badly bruised face.

She was on her knees putting some food into her dog's dish. Her dog is a rather large Mastiff. Anyway, as she was concentrating on putting the food into the dish, the mutt had head butted her - right in the mouth. The blow nearly knocked her out. She had a bit of trouble getting back up again. The incident left her a little light-headed. We thought she must've been a little light-headed buying a Mastiff when she wasn't used to dogs!

She didn't think anything more about it until the next morning. When she went into the bathroom first thing she saw her reflection in the mirror. Her lips were badly swollen and the area around her mouth was bruised. A bit like Goldie Hawn in *The First Wives Club* after she'd had Botox injections in her lips. Pam could only speak through clenched teeth because it was too painful to move her lips.

However, we set out on our walk. Pamela brought her apple with her. Brave of her really, considering it was going to take her the whole lunchtime to eat it. We headed up the hill from our building, past the car-park and along the dirt road towards the bushland. As we neared the bush we heard a commotion ahead of us.

We rounded the bend. There was a large blue-tongued lizard being attacked by two shiny black crows. He had thrown his tail off as a decoy, which is what blue-tongue lizards do they're when attacked. The tail was wriggling all over the place near him.

At the same instant we rushed towards the crows, shooing them away in an attempt to save the lizard from being eaten. After we'd chased them off, Pamela, who was still struggling with her apple said, 'Do you zink it wud like thum abble?'

'Well, you could give it some and see if it likes it,' we mumbled, not quite sure a blue-tongue lizard would eat apple. We thought they only ate snails and insects.

Pam's soft hear melted. She felt really sorry for the poor attacked reptile. Slowly biting off a small piece of apple, she held it between her thumb and forefinger, ready to give it to the injured lizard.

As she put her hand out with the peace offering, I swear to God, I've never seen anything like this EVER. That lizard lept at least one metre into the air and bit her on the finger. It latched on like a bull terrier, and it wasn't letting go for love or money. Pam screamed in pain. Waved her hand up and down, she tried to shake the lizard off. Up and down, up and down, up and down. Finally that feisty lizard finally let go on the up wave, and flew high into the air. Pam had quite a bit of hard waving going on by then. The blue-tongue hit the ground with a loud thwack.

All was quiet as we stood around and stared hard at the lizard on the ground. Surely he couldn't have survived such a horrific thud. He certainly looked dead. we stood around and stared at the poor tailless thing. Its legs were horizontal like he'd done the splits with both front *and* back legs.

Then we thought of poor Pam, with her bruised face and huge lips. AND now she had a sore finger as well. We murmured soothingly 'are you alright' 'did it pierce the skin'. 'Arr zay poinzonus?' she lisped through fat lips.

'NO,' I said. 'Don't think they're poisonous at all, but you should probably go to a Doctor and get some antibiotics. The bite might become infectious.'

Suddenly remembering the lizard, we turned around. Knock me down with a feather, he was gone! It must have scurried away. I would've too if I were him – and still alive.

We, on the other hand, walked back to work, vowing never to go for a walk up that hill again. It was just *too* traumatic. You could be scarred for life.

Tryptych - Jo Tregellis

A young teacher's accommodation experiences

1.

an attic room
in a country pub
cut lunch
hot breakfast and dinner
open fire
freezing cutlery...
too young for the ladies' lounge

2.

a room
in an old lady's house
near the railway station
narrow single bed
curtain-enclosed space
makes a wardrobe
all evening meals
pressure-cooked
kerosene heater
for very cold nights
pennies in the gas meter
for a shower

3.

another pub- quite old
with great hosts
in the Riverina
wonderful bacon and eggs...
old enough for the ladies' lounge
two beds in my room
one night
I swapped beds
next morning
great lumps of wall plaster
on my previous pillow

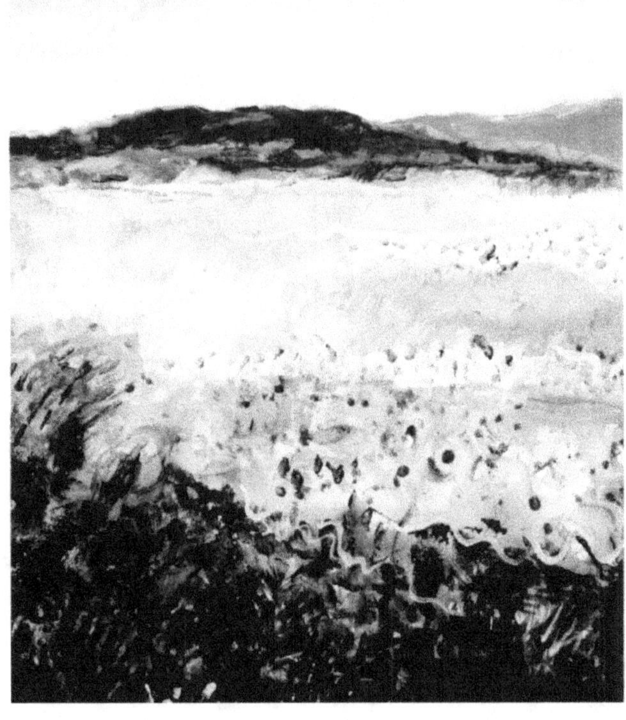

To our family, Wilsons Promontory is our most special place to visit and get away to. 'The Prom' holds many special memories for Peta and I. Wilson's Promontory is a two to three hour trip from Melbourne and sits at the southern edge of Victoria, jutting out into Bass Strait. More than twelve thousand years ago when sea levels were lower, indigenous Australians could travel from Wilsons Promontory across to Tasmania. The links were made through a range of low-lying land or islands. I have many words that describe the Prom.

Magnificent, beautiful, magical, peaceful, wild, untamed, serene, angry, humbling, exciting and unique. The Prom can be all these things in the space of an hour.

Parks Victoria manages Wilsons Promontory with Park Rangers having a special regard for the area. There are no motels, hotels, nightclubs or supermarkets. Accommodation can be obtained either by booking small cabins or units, or by bringing your tent or caravan onto one of the many camping areas. Camping site facilities are comfortable with running water and toilet/showers available. However, you need to bring everything with you as it can be fairly

Spartan. Most families camp out, but you need to book for major holiday seasons, and selections are usually done by lottery.

We've upgraded to a camper caravan. This gives us some comfort and allows us to support Adam more easily when camping. Leading up to the peak seasons we sometimes leave the van on site and travel between home and *The Prom*. Peta and I often come here individually during the year while one of us supports Adam at home. *The Prom* sometimes becomes my office. I can go on line with my phone modem and work directly from the van.

Adam's love of nature and the environment is especially finetuned at *The Prom*.

There are numerous walks and wildlife everywhere, in an area that's virtually untouched by humans, except for clearly defined manmade walking tracks. The weather can change dramatically as *The Prom* juts out into Bass Strait, so gales sweeping across the Strait score a direct hit to the camping area. It's not uncommon for entire campsites to be wiped out. Preparation is necessary—tents and anything else that could move must be securely tied down.

I remember one evening our brand new tent collapsed in a gale at midnight. Peta slept in the car, which shook all night. Adam and I slept in a small two-man tent that had survived the gale. The wind gusts were so strong that the tent roof was blown down onto our faces as we both tried to sleep. Adam thought this was great and laughed through the rest of the night.

In the 1990's a young boy, Paddy, wandered away from his family on a walking track near Lily Pilly Gully at *The Prom*. He was never found, despite the State spending days searching the area with bushwalkers and local aboriginal trackers. This tragedy made headlines around Australia at the time. Adam and I had met Paddy's mother several weeks before he was lost. Paddy had a disability. Adam and I had spent the evening with Paddy's mother at a demonstration in Melbourne - one of many where we requested more Government support for families. Adam wrote the following poem for Paddy's mother and sent after the tragedy.

LOVING - Dedicated to Paddy and his family.

Following tracks which are
away from those clearly defined
but finding nothing
the kid pads along in lost play,
wishing it will last forever as
warm days in summer.
Sadly and easily without warning,
aware of life's joys he
peers sweetly down and sees
pleasing sights.
Warmth departs from his weary self
as swiftly as it arrived.
Mum persists,
loving him more and hoping he lives
till found.
Lost he lives forever.
As time determines the awesome truth
that trapped as we all are
as weak and fragile beings,
what past nature gave us, a future too she gives.
As lots of people know.
Life is like a high and low sweet story,
with mum learning the warmth
of fellow man.
Loving everyone.
(The Prom – Les Cope)

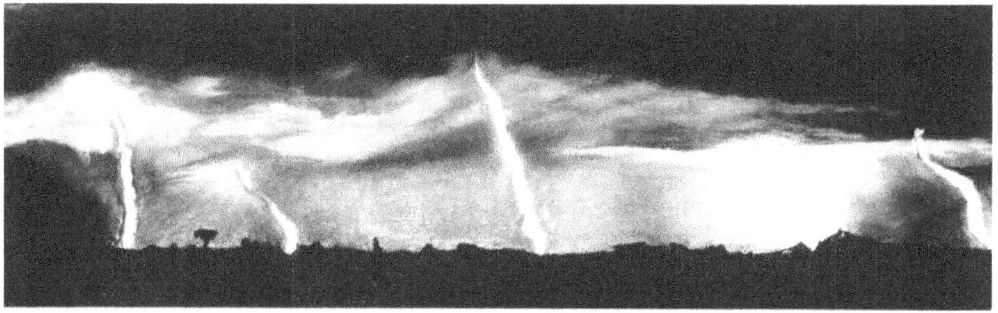

My youngest son, Bronson, has a tendency to be 'chaos on legs', but there was actually a time when we were caught in a National Disaster.

The electricity went out. This occurrence was usually attributable to neighbourhood kids, who seem to think vandalism of my property is either a national sport, or earns some kind of frequent flyer points. However, *this* time the electricity went out, the event coincided with the mother of all storms. My opinion, that at 1.00 am, it was useless to do anything, was not shared by Bronson, who never likes to let an opportunity to panic pass him by. There is *always* someone to phone. After all, he argues, many businesses have people on night shift who are bored. Sadly, I cannot lay scorn on this phrase as these are words straight out of my own mouth—when it suits me. Bronson, who can't remember anything associated with 'work', has an alarming tendency to repeat what I say verbatim; when it suits *him.*

Thunder crashed and lightning flashed simultaneously.

'There wasn't even a millisecond between the thunder and the lightning! You know what that means, Mum?' he yelled.

'Less sleep for me, more panic for you?'

'Sarcasm serves no useful purpose, Mum.'

'Maybe not for you, but I find it immensely satisfying.'

'Don't be stupid, Mum. This is serious.'

'It may or may not be, but I fail to see how joining you at Panic Stations will help anything.'

He then proceeded to inform me just how helpful I could be *if I chose.* Because Bronson has the tenacity of a colony of clams; I chose. We found an electricity account so he could relieve the boredom of the emergency call receiver.

'Geez, Mum, the whole of NSW is out!'

'For crying out loud Bronson, that's rubbish!'

He listed the suburbs, alphabetically, of course. Somewhere, there's a department in dire need of a boy with instant recall. Several minutes later he mentioned Wallsend. I began to panic. There were flash floods, medical emergencies and blackouts halfway up the coast.

'The woman said it might last days because it's so widespread,' Bronson informed me.

'Oh crap!'

Thankful for my large collection of candles, I started lighting them. Bronson could never sleep in the dark so the candles had to stay lit all night—meaning I couldn't go to sleep for fear of a fire. He was annoyingly refreshed in the morning and beginning to enjoy the adventure. Thunder and lightning had been replaced by the monotony of relentless, heavy rain. I watched as my carefully packed-down driveway flowed down the street, leaving rutted gullies that not even the Leyland brothers would attempt.

As soon as the stores opened, I set out on a hunt for batteries. Unfortunately, so had the rest of the state. There wasn't a single battery to be had for love or diamonds, which was just as well as I was short on both accounts. To top it off, it was June, smack in the middle of a bitterly cold winter. Bereft of his usual entertainments, Bronson decided to talk nonstop.

'What happens to people on life support?'

'Can we buy a wood fire?'

'Can we light a fire in the middle of the lounge room with old furniture?'

'Can we order batteries on the internet? Oh that's right, we can't use the computer.'

'Do we know anyone with a generator?'

'How long would it take to heat water in a saucepan with a candle?'

'What if we run out of candles?'

'What happens if looters come? What weapons have we got?'

'Why have you got your fingers in your ears, Mum? Don't ya know it's rude?'

We wore layers of clothes all day and night. Bronson went to spend the day with his father who had electricity. It grew dark. I cried. When he came home, I hugged him.

'I thought you were never coming home,' I whimpered, 'I thought you'd stay with your father and leave me to die alone in the cold.'

'Silly mother,' he said. 'I would never leave you to be alone and afraid, even for hot water, hot meals and a heater.'

I cried again and promised I would never put my fingers in my ears again.

That night the bitter chill worsened. At midnight Bronson had just nodded off. One of the candles flared a foot high. The cellophane surround was on fire. I rushed it to the sink and blew it out quickly. The deep well of melted wax splattered my hands with fiery liquid. Trying not to scream I quickly ran cold water over my hands. I painfully peeled the hardened wax from my blistered skin. I sat with the semi cool 'icepack' on my hands until morning. I tried to get out of the driveway to go for salve for my burns. The car sank six inches into the mud—and stayed. I looked up the road, but everyone was in the same situation.

Finally, after four days, the power was restored. My hands were still too sore to care about cleaning up the muddy patio or even looking at the disaster that had once been my back yard. I managed to get the car out by putting a couple of bricks under the front wheels. It was time for the claims process. I phoned the local insurance office. I was No. 28,749 in the queue. My call would be returned in the next millennium. At 3.00 am, I phoned Head Office. After all, everyone knows lots of businesses have bored people on night shift who don't mind the interruption. And they didn't. After sharing everything from life hints, recipes, good books to read and exchanging information on a variety of mental illnesses, all my claims were sorted.

(NT Storm – Louise Sauer)

A flock of white corellas swept in across the camping ground and settled in a tree not far from our campervan.

We were at Jabiru, in Kakadu National Park. It was July 2003, during the dry season. To start with, I took little notice of the corellas, but before long, I noticed something I found quite amazing. The birds were sitting quietly in a row on a long branch.

Nearby, there was a large sprinkler, which was rotating and watering the grass.

When the sprinkler rotated, the spray of water reached the tip of the overhanging branch where the corellas sat. There, one corella swung upside down, hanging from its feet, its wings widespread. The bird was having a shower, while the sun's rays shot coloured lights through the water droplets.

Before long, the corellas let go of the branch and flew back up to where the rest of the birds were perched. It settled on the branch next to the corella furthest from the water.

In the meantime, the corella at the other end of the line took its place under the spray, hanging under the branch, wings outspread.

About a minute later, that bird relinquished its place and also flew to the end of the queue, while the next one took its turn under the shower. Each time, the waiting birds would shuffle along the branch.

I watched for nearly half an hour. This courtly behavior was repeated again and again.

The sparkling white of the corellas contrasted with the clear blue sky, and the green of the tree. There were sixteen birds in the flock. Each bird's turn under the water lasted about a minute, and none took longer than another.

While the corellas perched patiently, awaiting their turn, they watched the bird under the water. Not one squabbled. There was no pushing or trying to jump their place in the queue.

In short, what I was observing was perfect British queuing behaviour in a flock of wild Australian birds!

Ocean Pools - Gail Hennessy

These pools, Oak Park baths, Shelley Beach baths and Newcastle Ocean baths are all Australian. All three are situated on the Pacific Ocean. Manmade, they have witnessed the 'learning to swim' experience of multitudes of Australians. Spaces of containment, they have been the first launching pad where many of us learnt mastery over the Australian surf. In this triptych I have used them as symbols as I have moved from tentative beginnings of testing myself in a sheltering pool to the wider world of body surfing through my adult life, and now in my senior years to the sustaining presence of the baths once again, albeit in a different location and by a different self.

<u>Triptych</u>

Oak Park Baths

I remember the day
I felt buoyancy
first thrill of freedom
from gravity's magnet

water the welcoming element
its maternal embrace
its liquid envelope
its silver-leaved presence

surge of the wave
a mentor
cradled
my five year old self
I can swim!

The Ocean Baths, Newcastle

A haven to stretch
arthritic limbs
salt water's buoyant blessing

I tread the sandy bottom
float on my back
seeking the placid blue

from the surf's tumble
I've graduated
to a playpen of still water

of self suspension
to enter this floating world
this fluid space of our dreams

Shelley Beach Baths

Thursdays in summer
were swimming days
for our convent school

in the boarder's dormitory
we changed between locker doors
we were taught modesty

we walked the esplanade
from Kinder to the Leaving
two by two

down to Shelley Beach.

In February's heat wave
we lined the shore
cheering on our teams

zinc cream painted our noses
we patterned the pool
with our barracking

they were shiny summer days
of salt and sand
of castles built in air

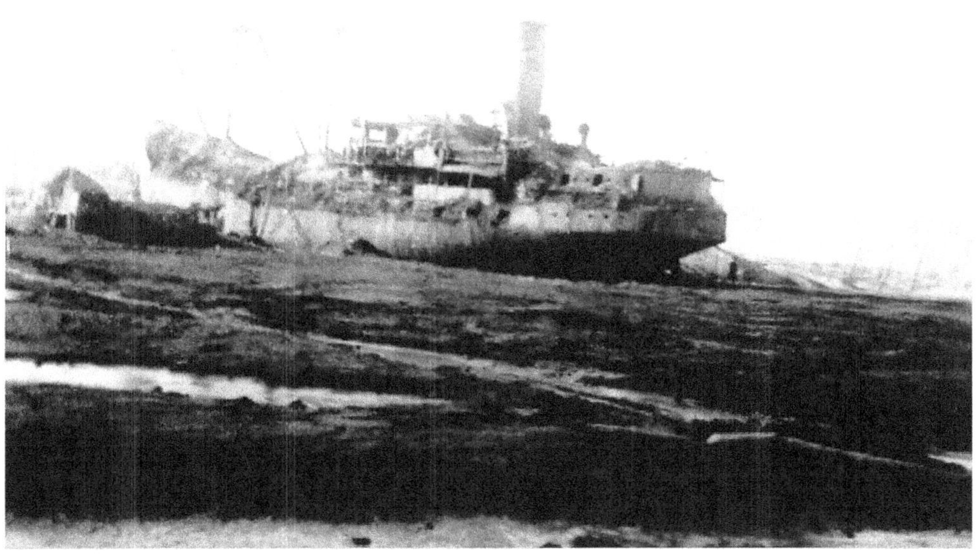

'I caught the S.S. 'Montoro' to Port Moresby, just like I told Alma, and within an hour, I was on the S.S. 'Duranbah' heading out to one of the islands. I worked as her second Radio Officer for one month. The day we arrived back in Port Moresby with our second load of copra, I was sent a message to report to W.R. Carpenter's office immediately with all my kit. When I arrived at their office in Mango Avenue, they informed me I was to report for duty on the S.S. 'Durour' as their Radio Officer had become ill and I was to replace him.'

'We sailed that very afternoon. We worked for six days and I received a message from W.R. Carpenter's again. The 'Durour' was to go into dry dock in four day's time at Karavia in Blanche Bay, Rabaul,' Jack recounted solemnly. He took a large gulp of beer and continued.

'Dry dock!' exclaimed Alma. The rest of the family all went, 'Ohhh!'

'Let him continue,' Bill said, waving him on.

'We'd been in dry dock for ten days and even though it sounds like an easy job, believe me supervising the natives was hard work! I was on deck the whole time. It was their job to grind off all the old paint, then prime and paint the hull—a huge task.

We took turns on watch 24 hours a day. The heat was unbearable. By the end of the first week, I was exhausted, like everyone else on board.' Jack looked around at the amazed faces. This was a fascinating story and no one interrupted. He had the floor.

'After ten days, the hull was finished and we were all looking forward to launching her back into the bay. It was Friday 28th May and we had to wait for the Captain, who'd gone to town. Around lunchtime, while I was sitting on the bridge deck, a whopping big earthquake occurred. I knew what it was as I'd felt them previously in New Zealand, but it frightened the life out of the others on board.'

'The 'Durour' jumped as though an explosion had gone off underneath her. She broke the chocks under the cradle she was balanced on, sliding up and down the rails as though she was on springs. Somehow, she managed to stay on the cradle, held only by the series of ropes which pulled her out of the water on to dry land.'

Alma, who had been quite indignant at him not even acknowledging that she had been left in limbo for more than nine months, was now very proud of him. Her father, Bill, was thinking this was going to be the most amazing story to tell at the pub the next day.

'A couple of hours later,' Jack continued, 'another moderate quake hit us, and after that quakes started coming every couple of minutes. There were only six of us on board. None of us got much sleep that night. Everyone aboard was very jittery. Straight after the first couple of quakes, most of the native boys had taken off.'

The family all moved in closer around the table so they didn't miss anything.

'After lunch on the Saturday, I was on deck, talking to the Slipway Manager. 'Fred,' I said to him, 'does Vulcan Island look lop-sided to you?" "Now that you mention it, it does look like it's tilted to one side by about six feet,' Fred replied.'

'Neither of us knew what it meant. It was strange to see an island that had been perfectly flat the day before and was now tilted out of the water 24 hours later.

'Fred asked the Chief Officer to put the ship into the water. The repairs had been completed and he was afraid of damage. However, the Chief Officer refused, as the Captain was still in Rabaul. Fred raced off the ship and drove off to get the Captain's permission.

'The ship's Doctor and I were intrigued with the reef, as it seemed to be rising up out of the harbour. We decided we'd get in the motor boat and go and investigate.

We took our two remaining native boys with us. We were cruising around the reef toward Rabaul, when suddenly the water became quite turbulent. I turned the boat around to head back to the ship. We were about four hundred yards from it and about two hundred yards from the shore, when the boys yelled out that the boat would soon be dry. For some reason the seabed seemed to have risen.'

Alma put her hand up to her mouth and cried 'What? Risen? Why?'

Gwen waved her hand and said, 'Oh, go on, go on.'

'It was weird to watch the seabed rise before our eyes, with fish flopping about and bits of coral popping up out of the sea. Moments before it was quite clear, and deep enough to take the draft of the motor boat. Then, about a hundred yards to the right, up spouted a column of smoke, steam and rocks. The noise was unbearably loud. Then to our horror, it came up in a series of spurts, higher and higher until we couldn't see the top for the smoke. Panic set in and we turned straight for the shoreline but before we had gone fifty yards, the boat was high and dry. A volcano was coming up out of the water right in front of our eyes!'

'A volcano!' they all spoke at once.

'I read about it in the Herald, but I thought you were out at sea, Jack,' Alma said in awe.

Jack took another mouthful of beer.

'By this time, the roar from the volcano was deafening. The others ran towards the beach, but I ran back to the 'Durour' to get my camera. I was now filthy dirty and covered in ash. My legs and arms were badly cut about from falling on the coral while running across the reef. I reached the ship, which was now covered in ash but high and dry. I quickly grabbed my camera and some film from my cabin, which was on the outer deck.'

'By now, the volcano had grown to a tremendous height, with small rocks falling all around the ship. I took all the photos I could in one minute, then decided it was time to get out of there. I jumped down off the ship and started jogging along the road away from the volcano, towards Kokopo. The heat was intolerable and seemed to be coming in waves from the volcano. I've never felt heat like it.' Jack shook his head.

'You're lucky to be alive, Jack,' Bill was amazed. Alma beamed, encouraging him.

'With the next explosion, I honestly thought we were done for, especially as now there were bolts of lightning flashing every few seconds. When the lightning hit the palm trees, they exploded into small fragments. It was just like shell fire. The noise was horrific. We were a small band of fifteen now, all running away from the volcano. The ash fallout was so heavy we were gasping for air. Our clothes were in tatters, we looked like ghosts, completely covered in a light grey powder.

'Just as we thought we couldn't walk one more step, who should turn up but Fred in his car. It was a miracle. His car was only a small runabout but we all piled in. We stood on the running boards or sat on the bonnet or the boot, wherever we could and he took all fifteen of us. Fred drove through ash for about five miles, along the coast road, until we were well clear of fallout. Fred stopped the car and we all got out. We sat down on the beach to watch the volcano in action.

'It was the most terrifying, yet wonderful sight any of us had ever seen or probably will ever see in our lifetimes. It was beyond words. There were clouds of ash and red hot rocks being thrown out of the top, interspersed with tremendous flashes of lightning and crashing thunder. The continuous noise almost numbed our senses.

'After a while, we climbed back into the car and drove to the Catholic Mission. They kindly supplied us all with clean clothes as ours were in shreds. We spent the night there. The earthquakes continued all night. None of us got any sleep.

'The next morning, many small schooners began to arrive in the harbour, bringing refugees from Rabaul. The American Steamer, 'Golden Bear', had managed to get out of the harbour at the first sign of the eruption on Saturday. It had gone around the other side of the peninsula from Rabaul and picked up refugees who'd walked around. I found out the 'Golden Bear's' radio operator had disappeared in the eruption so I offered to help out.

'I was the only means of communication to the outside world. I worked for four days as their Radio Operator. There was a pile of official messages and I only took naps when I was exhausted. The Captain of the 'Golden Bear' measured the volcanic cone using his sextant. It had grown six hundred and seventy feet high in the four days since the eruption started.'

Alma squeezed his hand. 'What happened, Jack? Why did it take all this time to get back?'

'The Captain asked me to stay on as the radio operator of the Golden Bear for about a week until all the refugees had been evacuated. Her radio officer never did show up and was presumed perished. The Captain asked me if I would take the ship to Hawaii for him. I was to be paid in American dollars and after we docked in Honolulu, they would send me back to Sydney on a passenger liner, First Class. I had a lovely cruise back on the S.S. Monterey.' Jack grinned.

'Wow, first class, what was that like, Jack?' Gwen asked admiringly.

'Everything was so elegant and the highest quality. I brought Alma a copy of one of the dinner menus,' Jack said pulling it out of his top pocket and proudly handing it to her.

'Wow, the food sounds delicious. And free wine! Did you have to pay for this food Jack?' Alma asked amazed and then handed it round the table for all to see.

'Not a penny. It was all included in my fare home. It was the best thing that ever happened in my whole life. The 'Monterey' Radio Officer invited me into his radio room and showed me the equipment, which was all the very latest. They treated me like a king and I'm not embarrassed to say, I liked it enormously,' Jack chuckled.

'This whole story sounds like it could be made into a movie, doesn't it, Essie?' Bill said.

'I've never heard anything like it in my whole life! What an amazing adventure, although I'm not jealous of being there when the volcano came up out of the water,' Estelle said shaking her head.

'Jack, I can't imagine how frightening it would have been with the noise and the ash and having to walk miles through it. You're lucky to be alive,' Alma gazed into his intense blue eyes.

'Yes, I do consider myself one of the lucky ones. Anyhow, I must go now or I will miss the last train. Alma, will you walk me to the gate?' Jack said, smiling at her. He took his leave from the family and, after closing the front door behind them, Jack took Alma in his arms and gave her a tender kiss. Alma put her arms around his neck. 'Darling, I'm so sorry I didn't get time to write to you, but you know now why it was impossible.'

'I was so worried about you, Jack. You never missed writing before. But somehow I knew you were alright. I just wondered why it was taking you so long to come home.'

'I love you Alma.'

'I love you too Jack. Time just dragged while you were away.'

The following Saturday afternoon, Jack turned up at their house. He found Alma down the back yard, doing laundry. She wore an apron and her hair was tied up in a scarf, because of the steam from the copper. Spotting him as he walked across the yard, she stood up, wiping her hands on her apron.

'Darling, good news. I've just landed a job with Civil Aviation. It's a Government job and I won't have to go back on the ships anymore. I'm to be sent to Townsville for five months.'

'Townsville! That's so far away,' Alma exclaimed in despair. Not again, she thought.

He grabbed her hand and got down on one knee.

'Will you marry me, darling? You know I love you. I want you to come to Townsville with me. What do you say?' He reached into his pocket and opened a small box. Inside was a solitaire diamond ring in a filigree platinum setting.

Alma threw her arms around him.

'Yes, oh yes.'

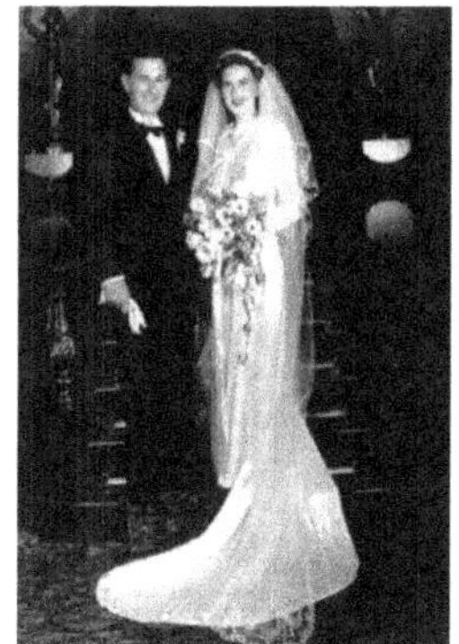

This is a true story. My parents married and lived in Townsville for five years during WWII. My father was OIC at Townsville Airport for the duration of the war.

(Family photos – Roslyn Jewel)

Rivers of Life - Linda Visman

As the first raindrops fall,
the red desert earth releases
the sharp, clean smell of ozone.
I lift my face to taste
the heaven-sent drops;
to receive their cleansing baptism,
their cool anointing
on my thirsty, sun-dried skin.

The long-awaited build-up,
the sultry grey-black promise
of summer storm-clouds,
is finally, thunderously, fulfilled
in the unrelenting barrage
of a season-breaking downpour;
a cascade that quenches
the sky's glowing furnace.

At once I am drenched.
Coolness trickles from head to toe;
washing away the summer dust.
My feet are lost in red-brown mud,
as tiny rivulets unite, to form
streams that expand into
shallow, brush-dotted lakes,
through which I splash.

Earthy waters, fed by heaven's bounty,
surge along winter-dried river-beds
that Rainbow Snake their way
through sandy, spinifex plains
and the rocky, spirit-haunted gorges
of Australia's red-ochred heart.
These surging, foaming torrents
irrigate a vast desert land,
carrying with them a sacrament,
the annual rebirth of the land.

At season's end the rivers pass away,
buried beneath those thirsty sands.
Then, almost as I watch,
multitudes of waiting seeds,
aroused by the redeeming waters,
erupt into life, and carpet the red soil
in white and mauve and gold.
In weeks, they too will fade away,
until the next rainy season brings once more
the ozone smell of nature's baptism.

Christmas

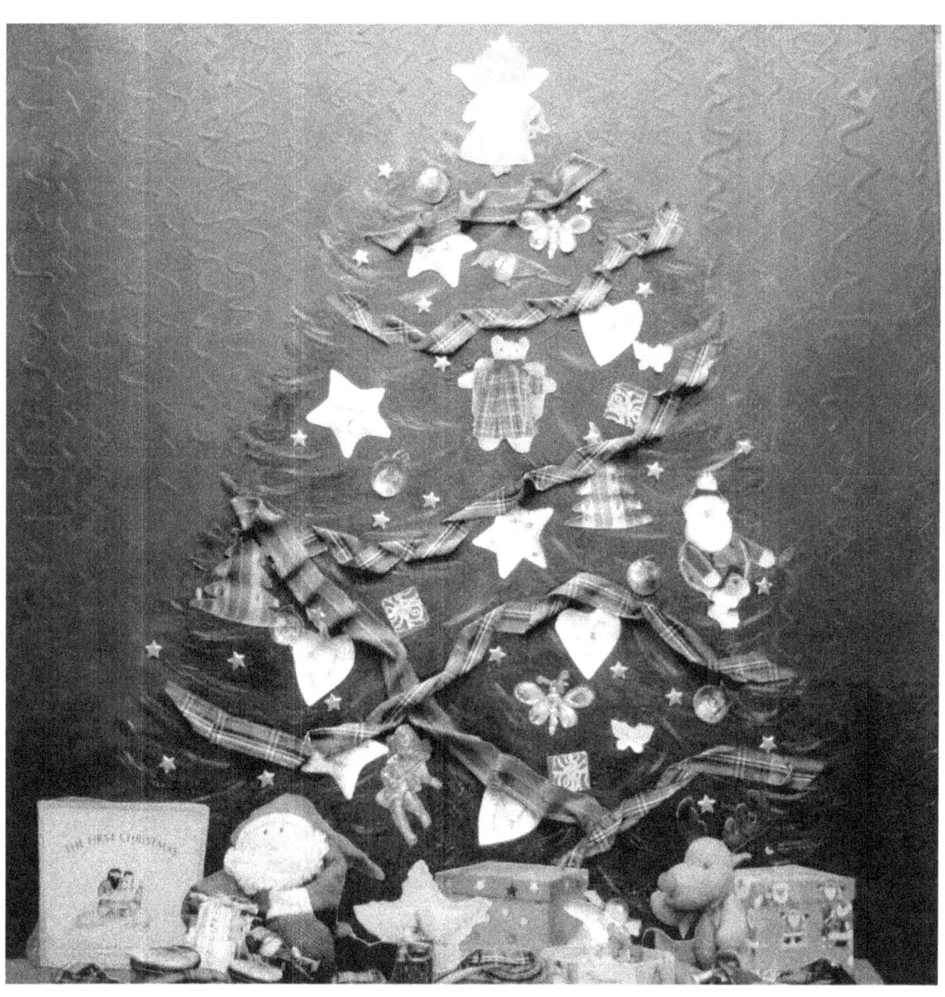

♫ ♫ *'Jingle bells, jingle bells, jingle all the way, Oh what fun...' ♫ ♫*

'Will one of you blooming nurses turn off that blasted Christmas music!' says Harry. 'There's only s'posed to be twelve days of Christmas, but the way *this place* has been windin' things up, ya'd think there were twelve 'undred.'

'Somebody got out of the wrong side of the bed,' mutters Marj.

Cathy steps in to ask Harry how many eggs he wants on his toast. She has been a nurse long enough to know that Christmas isn't all joy and gladness. Especially not here, in the nursing home. This simple question is enough to sidetrack Harry into his daily argument that the scrambled eggs 'they serve in this place aren't real eggs—they're powdered'. He says this loudly enough so that Meg, the cook, also long accustomed to the tirades of young and old, merely rolls her eyes.

'Back in England...' says George.

'Oh 'ere 'e goes again,' mutters Harry. 'Banging on about 'Mother England'.'

'...we had a white Christmas every year. Nothing like it really. Just doesn't seem like Christmas without snow,' continues George, who holds no animosity towards Harry and politely passes him the strawberry jam. After all, it was George who found Harry swearing his head off earlier this morning when the clerk delivered yesterday's mail from the Admin office. Harry had opened a gift-wrapped parcel containing two new pair of pyjamas and was throwing them in the nearest bin.

'Not your size, Harry?' George had enquired politely, as he wheeled his chair alongside Harry.

'Hmmph,' Harry stuffed the pyjamas and wrapping further down the bin with his walking stick.

'S'me blasted son. Hasn't spoken t'me fer twenty years, then this.'

George nodded wisely.

'Have a minor stroke and some idiot *informs 'im...'* Harry raised his voice pointedly in our direction. '...next thing ya know, he thinks a bloke's ready to kick the bucket and sends pyjamas! Left his run too late, he has.'

'The nurse at the hospital phoned him, Harry. You know that,' I explained.

'S'none of their blasted business. Dunno how his phone number got onta me notes.'

'It's done now, Harry. Done and dusted,' offered George.

'Too right mate. Done-in and in the dustbin.' He laughed at his own joke.

'Wonder what he would have bought if you had a *major* stroke,' murmurs George, still fascinated at the image of the striped pyjamas among the food scraps.

'Probably a satin smokin' jacket, a lawyer and a pair of flaming slippers, I'd reckon mate.'

After working many Christmas Days there's nothing new to see here. Mabel paces at the window waiting for her family even though they aren't coming until 11.30—just before lunch, and it now only 8.00 am. We only manage to get her to eat breakfast by telling her she'll ruin Christmas if she doesn't eat, because she'll pass out from low blood sugar and end up not being able to go out with her nieces. She isn't a diabetic, but her sister Betty suffered from it and died of renal complications connected to the disease only last year.

After breakfast Marj chats with Beatrice while Ethel fusses in her purse. Harry and George move towards the front door for their early morning 'constitutional', making sure none of the confused patients escape as they leave. Harry opens the door wide enough for George's wheelchair.

Cathy, John and I exchange rueful smiles. John turns the music off, announcing he's 'had enough Christmas spirit to last another decade'. A quick flick of the cassette player and Bing Crosby singing White Christmas dies a sudden death.

'At least it's we three and Meg this year, 'I say to John. 'Last year was hell with that manic kitchen-hand having never worked in this wing and having an agency nurse who didn't know one end of the place from the other.'

'Yep, just us 'old hands',' John responds as he automatically picks up Emily's walking stick, while she bats her eyes at him.

'You have to stop spoiling her, John. You know she does that on purpose.'

'Oh, don't tell me. I know. She thinks she's twenty one and out on the town.' His forehead creases in a frown which still manages to show his unflappable good humour.

There's an urgent ringing of the front door alarm. I look up to see Evangeline Foster with her rather irate looking son Paul standing beside her at the double glass entrance. I throw John and Cathy a knowing glance and they look away to hide their laughter. Evangeline looks a little dishevelled and disoriented. Her son just looks cranky.

He grips her overnight bag with a white knuckled hand. Evangeline glides regally through the foyer and goes to sit beside Beatrice. She immediately starts chatting about the weather as if nothing is amiss. Evangeline was supposed to stay with her family for four days. She's only been gone overnight. I had tried to tell her son Paul, and his elegant wife Sylvia, on their infrequent visits, that Evangeline was often confused, especially at night – but they had greeted my efforts with a dismissive wave. 'Mother's fine *with us*,' Sylvia had claimed smoothly at the time, treating us to one of her 'superior looks'.

'My wife Sylvia...' Paul began.

'Top lofty, that one,' says Evangeline loudly to her seatmate. I cringe. Cathy turns the music back on to cover John's spurt of laughter. And probably whatever other confidences Evangeline will choose to share. She loves an audience.

I look outside to the darkened windows of the BMW. It appears Sylvia has more important things to do than return 'Mother'. I calmly look Paul in the eyes—waiting. I'm enjoying this, but trying not to show it. He will baulk at any questions, but if I stand here quietly he'll feel obliged to say something by way of explanation. He's polite that way.

'*She...*' he begins again, pointing in Evangeline's direction, who is blithely ignoring her firstborn's existence, '...*she* got up during the night, drunk the sherry for Santa, ate the biscuits for the reindeers, and then opened all the children's presents. We woke up to the kids wailing, paper everywhere and her...*tipsy!*'

I hear John choking. My face wrestles to remain passive. 'Please stop Paul', I think, 'I can't hold this in much longer'. I start saying my four times tables and avoid looking at him.

'...then...*you won't believe this.*' He pauses. I'm in agony. 'She packs all the toys in her suitcase and says 'I want to go home—*home—for crying out loud*', where the hell did she think she was?'

I can't speak. I dare not move a muscle. Thankfully Paul requires no response, and through his own heightened opinion of himself, assumes he sees understanding in my eyes. I deserve an Oscar. He thumps the suitcase down, rushes to his car and takes off, slewing gravel in the car park. Cathy, John and I explode at exactly the same moment.

There is a hush over the laden table—set for 13 instead of forty. The tinsel hangs crookedly. Cathy gives it a searching look, mutters 'pfft', then walks to the table. We have served the patients their Christmas dinner, and I have decided that today the staff will join them. So there we sit, at one long table, with all the trimmings and trappings of Yuletide. Bon-Bons, lollies, pudding, gifts and a colourful array of hats.

Evangeline sits with Beatrice, her hair now perfectly coiffed, although she claims to have 'an appalling headache'. Harry and George can't pull the Bon-Bons apart so they enlist John to tussle with me to break them open. Then we hand out the paper jokes and toy animals. The men read the jokes, claim they're 'a load of old rubbish', then entertain us all with their own versions of the 'best of the best jokes of all time'. They're funny and it's infectious.

I look down the two rows. It's different from the traditional image of Christmas. There are feeding aids, special plates and walking aids. Cathy stops for a second to prevent Merv eating the serviette he's just buttered. I smile. Real Christmas comes in all sizes. 'Family' comes in all shapes. And home...well home, can be anywhere.

Anywhere at all.

How far is it to Christmas? - Jo Tregellis

How far is it to Christmas?
I was there once
full of midnight mass
and candle's glow
carolling with gusto -
after communion
all was golden
a congregation cocooned in reverence.

How far is it to Christmas?
I was there once
my eyelids screwed in feigned sleep
ears hearing santa sounds
then riding the fabled scooter
down dream hill
on solid tyres.

How far is it to Christmas?
I was there once,
a huge chook bought on tick
baked by a little mother
presented on our one large platter,
from corner to corner
on the ceiling

our chained streamers
made from coloured magazine strips
and flour glue
danced over us.
How far is it to Christmas?
I think too far,
and if the memory is lost
can I get back
the warmth of mother's cuddles,
the laughter of little brother or
the fragrant delight of a new book
and the comfort of belonging?

On the Dot - Magdalena Ball

Rudolph's nose warps blue at Doppler shift lightspeed through Christmas
eve sky.

Young scientist tosses bedcovers
zero dimension
the point of stocking fill
compression
big bang impending
while he dreams better physics
a future gleamed beyond the promise of
tomorrow.

Nothing doesn't always come from nothing.

His rapid eye movements
trace fibre optic lights
around the tree
putting a name on 300,000 species
living organisms yet to be classified.

Neurotransmitter stimulation
outweighs the sweet load of Christmas lollies
waiting for morning
like the discovery of
one dimensional symmetry
a quantum dot
lightning strike
jingle bell memory
ready for dawn's wake
to face down the overflow
producer, consumer hunger

false tokens of love
with crayons and brushes
of fresh wonder
make something new.

While Sally watched her children chasing each other around the partly decorated tree, squealing and laughing, she reflected on the last year and how it turned out to be the best Christmas ever. She had been broke and so was her sister Brenda.

Between the two single mothers they had four children who were getting IOU's instead of presents.

The sisters emptied money boxes and withdrew the few dollars in their bank accounts, pooling their money as they had done so many times as siblings growing up. Together they held a family meeting to work out a method to get the best day for $32.15.

Having decided on the beach, that's free, they caught a bus to Swansea to save on petrol. Their packed lunch was food they had voted the three favourites, prawns, mangoes and ice-cream, choc-chip of course.

It was a hot and sticky day and it wasn't long before the kids were hot and sticky too, mango juices washed from their faces and hands by the warm salty sea.

They found a shady spot to rest after eating, the cousins playing Scrabble with Brenda as Sally pretended to read her novel. She was really studying her family. She saw with pride and admiration how between them the family had made what could have been a sad and disappointing Christmas into one of great joy.

Topping their day was the return trip on the bus, where the driver was dressed as Santa and played Carols. He encouraged them all to join in and the little group sang the loudest. He detoured to a street with the brightest lights and the children put their Christmas change in the wishing well for the Salvos. They had had a great day and didn't need the few coins left over.

Oh, there was joy in the world that day, Sally reflected.

Now tomorrow, that's something else!

The Christmas Pudding - Jennifer Goard

This Christmas was going to be hot, hot, hot, hot, and like so many other Aussie families, it was our turn to host the family Christmas day – with compulsorily mid-day meal and decorations to boot. We had set up the function outside under the spreading arms of the Desert Ash, as my house was just too small to hold so many people including all the kids. This fabulous tree, which stood in the middle of our backyard, would be the roof for our festive hall the green leaves symbolic of Christmas and we figured it would be very pleasant sitting in the shade tucking into our dinner, rather than being stifled by the heat that built up inside the house during the day.

All morning I had been madly dashing backwards and forwards preparing stuff. Like a desperate chook running around without a head – for that is what I had become – at last had everything ready to go for when our respective relatives arrived. For two full weeks leading up to the event I had organised chickens and salads, fruit to be made into platters and many desserts like strawberries which had to be dipped in chocolate Christmas morning.

As custom would have it, the family were bringing their bits and pieces to add to the table too. My sister always made her baby spinach salad with the crunchy noodles which tasted great and my sister–in-law always brought along her world famous (in Melbourne), strawberry cheesecake, which went down brilliantly. Everyone brought their choice of 'poison' to drink, but the piece de resistance, was my parents' plum pudding. Mum and Dad had a tradition. Starting in March they would concoct the largest amount of pudding mixture possible, throwing into the cauldron a variety of secret ingredients, - enough to feed all of the starving people of Africa - and create the biggest Christmas plum pudding in the history of the world.

After making the planet sized pudding, they would place it into calico cloth and hang it in the laundry to dry. Whatever was left of the mixture was usually enough for three little satellite puddings which were the personal ones for my siblings and me to have later. These little puddings were hung up next to the big one in mum's laundry looking like the moons of Jupiter.

The sun blazed down out of a brilliant azure sky as the people started to arrive.

Kisses and hugs were given at the door as one by one the families of our family entered our house, bearing armfuls of food and presents galore. These were dutifully placed under the decorated Christmas tree in the lounge room on their way through to the backyard.

When the mob had all arrived the adults got stuck into the wine which loosened tongues inducing them to tell their stories about what had occurred to them over the year. The kids ran around chasing our dog amongst the trestle table. The adults seated on deck chairs under the Desert Ash all in their colourful summer clothes, looked just like the wrapped up presents under the fake tree in the lounge room.

It was a casual affair. The main meal was a smorgasbord of cold meats and salads of various degrees depending on which lettuce was used. These had been laid out in bowls and plates on the table, and everyone helped themselves to the fare. We were stuffed with food, drink, laughter and conversation as the day slowly wore away. The shadow from the tree stretched further across the yard towards the western fence, and the heat from the day was tagging along behind. It was time for the main event, the lighting of the pudding, Bombe Alaska style. This had been billed - by my parents' assurances - as the highlight of the day. Christmas would dissolve into nothing if this pudding, lovingly made and held in reverence in the laundry, were not covered in brandy and lit with a match, creating an ambient blue fire, making all present in awe of it.

With much fanfare, hoo-ha, and adulation from the assembled crowd, the pudding was triumphantly brought forth from the kitchen where it had been steaming in boiling water. It was carried out into the back yard and placed on the decorated Christmas trestle table. A long-winded speech was given by my Dad on the exhausting year he and Mum had endured tending to the cherished pudding, and on the process of making it. With bated breath we watched as he poured the brandy over the confection, struck the Redhead that flamed next to it.

Absolutely nothing happened. A disappointed sigh swept among the onlookers when the pudding failed to burst into a flaming inferno. Another match was lit with the same result. We wondered about the outcome. The pudding must be lit somehow or all our work was for naught.

My husband had a brilliant idea - often the case during moments of complexity such as this. Addressing the assembled family members he informed us he knew how to save the moment. He disappeared into his shed with a smile that said he was 'up to something'. He emerged with a blow torch and gas cylinder attached. He fired it up, aiming it at the pudding, much to my mum's horror. The beloved pudding was scorched in a fiery hell. We broke into laughter, a sense of 'the ridiculous' took over. At least it was on fire! And how! Definitely time to put the bloody thing out, before the table and everything within cooee caught fire. I must say, even though there was a bit of crunchy charcoal crust the pudding tasted great with custard and ice-cream.

We soon decided it was time to go in. Shuffling inside the tiny house we sat anywhere we could, seats, the floor, extra chairs brought in from outside, the arms of chairs. Some stood in doorways looking in - we were family sharing a tiny room to watch the joy in people's faces as they each gave and received presents. Everyone was grateful and happy to share the day.

The shadows lengthened outside, as the sun set over the western fence. People moved away, back home with their cache of goods and Christmas moved out the front door with them.

Phew! We could all relax now; the big day was over until next year.

Christmas - Gail Hennessy

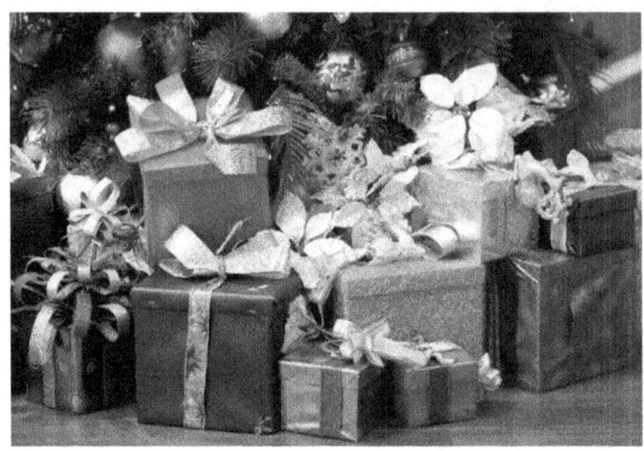

I return
to the place I was born
the short street running
downhill to the ocean

indigo blue in winter
scarred by white foam
over the water the boat line jut
of Bundeena's shoreline.

The scurf grey of tea tree
bushland where I crouched
to watch the busy ants
ferry sugar beads I fed them.

Outcrop of rock, a striated shelf
cradling Oak Park swimming pool.
I walk to school along the esplanade
dreaming into lateness.

Cross-over curtains in the kitchen
the dresser marshalled with plates
canisters atop announced
the uncertainty of labels.

I can touch
that room's hearth
the stove demanding shovelfuls
of pre carbon diamonds.

My mother's coal black hair
as she rose from the oven
with scones in pungent steam
baked on Sundays for my grandmother.

Mondays she strings the ghosts of washing
along the clothesline as I spread
handkerchiefs on the kikuyu,
ginger beer ferments in the laundry.

In the weeks before Christmas she buys
bottles of orange, lemonade, lime
fizzy drinks that are hoarded
along with muscatels, nuts and presents.

In the New Year we catch the train
into the city to pay off the loan
that has ransomed us to Christmas…

CONTRIBUTORS

Linda Brooks This collection has come from Linda's vision of historic narrative as bold and full-bodied. Her sideways slant on life brings wicked humour and sharp characters. She authored a childhood memoir *An Australian Childhood*, fiction novels and several illustrated children's books. Visit—www.lindaruthbrooks.com

Magdalena Ball is a gently flowing river, with a mind that is flexible and scary smart. Magdalena runs *The Compulsive Reader*. She is the author of the poetry book *Repulsion Thrust*, the novel 'Sleep before Evening' and several other books.

See: www.magdalenaball.com

Christina Batey always has a smile on her face. She exudes warmth and enthusiasm. Her style is effortless, whimsical and crisp. She has written a teen novella *Kicker*. What Christina needs is more time. With three children and a busy life, free time would be like winning the lottery!

Louise Berry has a mind as quick as a steel trap. Her subtle style of observing life is reflected in all her writing. A unique knowledge of human life and experience makes Louise a valuable contributor.

Julie Cochrane has the kind of warmth that permeates on a cold night. Considered, weighing her words and responses, she is also spontaneous. Her words get to the heart of life's experiences.

Les Cope is focused, professional and warm-hearted. Calm and diligent, yet artistic and insightful. He is lobbyist. He creates - art, words and designs website. Visit his site:
http://www.copeart.com.au

Jennifer Goard lives in the bayside suburb of Bonbeach, Melbourne. She uses the surrounding waters of Port Phillip and Westernport bays as her playground, and this is reflected in her art. She is an artist, and has had many successful exhibitions. Visit her website www.jendatrading.com.au

Jo Hanrahan has lived a full and colourful life. She has travelled and studied culture and language. With her origins firmly grounded in the Australian bush, her writing is uniquely Aussie.

Gail Hennessy has been reading and writing all her life and her short stories and poetry have been published in newspapers and journals since the '70's. Her book of poems 'Witnessing' is a collection that brings together published and new poetry in a loosely autobiographical history.

Roslyn Jewel is indomitable, buoyant and fearless. Well why shouldn't she be? After all, she can do anything! When she isn't rescuing her partner, she's scrubbing graffiti off her fence or looking for another house to renovate. With a story to die for, we only hope she'll find the time to finish it.

John McBride is full of s**t. He claims he swam the Murray River from length to length. He taught Julia Gillard how to box, and he climbed Ayres Rock with his bare teeth. Don't listen to anything he says; but read his stories—they bite. His contact details are: **j.mcbride@internode.on.net**

Victoria Norton delights in life and all its mysteries. With a background in health care, people have always fascinated her. Victoria is putting her high school English teacher on notice...Mrs K...the blockbuster novel is on its way!

Rina Robinson is a combination of charm and childlike zest for life. This is reflected in her stories, which always have hidden surprises. Her fantasy novellas contain all these things and more. A skilful narrator, Rina weaves her characters with warmth and vitality.

Louise Sauer has the unenviable talent of going in ten directions at once--and damned well succeeding. Her art is subconscious, rare, brilliant and intuitive.

Jo Tregellis is a masterful poet. Her work is measured and enduring. Poetry is as natural as breathing to Jo, and as perfect as a science. Many of her poems have won awards and she has been widely published. Her poetry evokes visual imagery that is clear, fresh, authentic and thought-provoking.

Linda Visman migrated from England as a child. A country girl. Living and teaching in remote areas of Central Australia brought an appreciation of life in all its variety. She is hoping an astute publisher will realise what a gem her children's novel is, and publish it – but she's not holding her breath!

Matthew Glenn Ward could talk underwater and has probably tried to. His mind is mercurial and always moving, like ripples on a lake. He's nocturnal, day-urnal and any-urnal he can be, but as a professional he is a masterful, organised, presenter of workshops. See his work at www.matthewglennward.com

www.ingramcontent.com/pod-product-compliance
Lightning Source LLC
Chambersburg PA
CBHW080446030726
47592CB00011B/2993